Beyond Betrayal

No More Broken Churches

Mark Wargo

Copyright © 2015 by Mark Wargo.

All rights reserved. Written permission must be secured from the publisher to use or reproduce any part of this book, except for brief quotations in critical reviews or articles. The use of short quotations or occasional page copying for personal or group study is permitted and encouraged.

Scripture quotations taken from the
Amplified® Bible,
Copyright © 1954, 1958, 1962, 1964, 1965, 1987 by The Lockman Foundation
Used by permission." (www.Lockman.org)

THE HOLY BIBLE, NEW INTERNATIONAL VERSION®, NIV® Copyright © 1973, 1978, 1984, 2011 by Biblica, Inc.™ Used by permission. All rights reserved worldwide.

Scripture taken from the New King James Version®. Copyright © 1982 by Thomas Nelson, Inc. Used by permission. All rights reserved.

Scripture quotations from The Authorized (King James) Version. Rights in the Authorized Version in the United Kingdom are vested in the Crown. Reproduced by permission of the Crown's patentee, Cambridge University Press

Contact Information:

Waller Hill Publishing, LLC
P.O. Box 493
Tennille, GA 31089
www.wallerhill.com

10 9 8 7 6 5 4 3 2

Thank you to my beautiful bride of over 23 years. You are a rock and I couldn't imagine doing this without you. I love doing life and ministry with you! Thank you for all the love, encouragement and for the hours and days you put into my 'much-needed' edits throughout this book.

Thank you to the most awesome staff on the planet Doug, Carrie, Jeff, Alaine, Sarah, Laura, Cory and the rest of our great team; thank you for moving the kingdom of God forward with us. We are blessed by the friendships and for all you have sacrificed to bring change. We are honored to serve with you, and we know that greater things have yet to come!

Thank you to Cross Current Church for staying the course. I pray we always have the heart to continue loving Jesus, loving each other and building the unity within. May we always be a people of Grace, Generosity and Gratitude. Our best days are ahead!

Thank you to all my former pastors for playing the role you did in helping me grow and become who I am today. I'm forever grateful to these men who have taught me so much: Pastor Skip Higgins, Pastor Sam Woodard, Pastor Harvey Hester, Pastor Chad Waller, Pastor Randall Gearhart and Pastor Michael Hindes. Thank you!!

Finally, thank you to Wall-Hill Publishing for supporting this book and for believing in it! What a blessing you are.

Foreword

There is a lot of talk about the brokenness of the church today with seemingly few offering hope for how it can be different. Yet it still remains that the church is the only institution that Christ said He had plans to build on the earth. It behooves us to learn how to do this correctly and to stop hurting people in the process.

In this book, Mark Wargo not only identifies some of the problems facing the church, but he also offers solutions and hope for the church to stop this cycle. He clearly takes us on a path through the painful experiences of betrayal and difficult lessons he learned as a young pastor, bringing a church out of a tail spin of destruction back to a place of being a life-giving force in their community.

I do not know anyone more qualified to write this book than Mark Wargo. When we met him and Tracee almost 23 years ago, I had no idea of the journey we were about to embark on–and what a journey it has been. Mark and Tracee have been some of the most faithful and steady ministers of the gospel that Melinda and I have ever had the privilege of serving with. They portrayed perhaps more clearly than anyone I have ever seen the quality of God that just doesn't give up-even when others around them did. They remained faithful to the mission God had given them and watched God do amazing things on their behalf.

For the sake of full discloser, I am a huge Mark Wargo fan. I love this man and his family. They have been some of the most faithful friends we have ever known. Even though betrayal, much as this book describes, tried to destroy our friendship, we trusted God for restoration, and God did just that-He restored one of the most amazing friendships I have ever had. I could not be more proud of Mark and am honored to call him my friend.

This is not an easy read, but rather a book that will challenge you to the core. I cannot recommend it strongly enough to you. Have you been betrayed? Do you feel broken? Read this book... and hold on because you are about to plunge head first into some truth that will usher you into a new freedom and complete healing if you allow it. If you see yourself in these pages as having the qualities of a betrayer, REPENT! Cry out to God to set you free. Deal with your hurts and find freedom. There is much kingdom work to be done and, we all need to get on with it!

Let's work together as the body of Christ to stop the brokenness, stop hurting each other and rise together, declaring hope and declaring no more broken churches!

Chad Waller
Lead Pastor of VC2
CEO of Waller-Hill Publishing
Tennille, Georgia

Table of Contents

Intro	11
I Love The Church	19
Who Are They?	31
Absalom-Style Betrayers	41
Delilah-Style Betrayers	73
Judas-Style Betrayers	87
Getting Through Betrayal	99
Three Headed Monster	111
Personal Agendas	119
Selfish Ambitions	139
Control Issues	147
We Can Beat It	161
Getting Beyond Betrayal	183
Will You Be The One?	199

Intro

We will be betrayed even by parents, brothers and sisters, relatives and friends, and they will put some of you to death.
- Luke 21:16

At that time many will turn away from the faith and will betray and hate each other.
- Matthew 24:10

Probably not the most ideal way to begin a book, but I just thought I'd begin with some light-hearted scriptures and encouraging words from Jesus (feel the humor). These are just some of the promises we can hold onto as we follow him. These words are what Jesus personally spoke to his disciples long ago and words that I believe he still speaks to His followers today. In the first passage, He warns us of who the betrayers in our lives will be, and in the second passage, He explains why betrayal will exist in the first place.

The reason for betrayal, especially within our churches, is simple - people fall away. They fall away from Jesus, the truth, His grace and His love. What is interesting to note is that the betrayal we experience more times than not will come from people who are connected to us, a church, and to the Lord. These are people who fall away and disconnect, and the results are devastating. Here are just some of the results that betrayal has caused: broken relationships, families, marriages, dreams, goals, teams, businesses, and sadly...churches. Betrayal is ugly and I don't believe it is going away. I believe betrayal will continue to increase with every generation who remains disconnected from Jesus. Sadly, if the trend continues, betrayal will become the norm of our society, and we will see even more broken lives. But does betrayal have to continue within our churches?

It is extremely saddening to see how much betrayal is in the world today, but what is really disheartening is how much betrayal happens within the local churches throughout the world. My heart does break when I see the staggering statistics of how many pastors monthly are leaving their callings and how many people are disengaging from the awesomeness of the 'church.' I realize not all this is related to betrayal, but much of it is. This is not what the church was created for. The painful betrayal that has led to numerous broken churches is taking its toll, and now we have too many disengaging and not connected at all.

You know, I guess in my early ministry days, I was a little naive. Actually, to be quite honest, I was a lot naive! Somewhere in the back of my brain I felt that if I were doing the right things such as serving, loving, and praying, then for the most part it would be smooth sailing. I mean I knew I'd have to face some challenges, but I never dreamed I would have to deal with the issues and betrayals as I have over the years. I never dreamed that betrayal would be so much a part of my life and especially while being a part of the church. Truth be told, I never gave it much thought. At some level I expect betrayal from people outside of the church, but what I'm surprised at is the number of people inside the walls of the church who do betray - Senior pastors betraying their staff and the congregations they are leading, support pastors betraying their pastors, worship leaders betraying their pastors, lay leaders betraying their senior pastor and creating church splits, people betraying people. We all know it happens, but why? Why does it happen? What can we really do about it? Well, I'm glad you asked! I'll answer these questions and more throughout the book, and I do believe there are answers.

Years ago, I was in the middle of a betrayal by a very close friend. We had served several years together in ministry, and one day, it all came to a close. The jealousy, lies and behind-the-back scheming changed everything and wounded many people...including me. One day, while I was in the scriptures researching and studying on this great and uplifting topic of betrayal (insert chuckle), I couldn't believe all that the Bible had to say on it. Some things I had read a number of times throughout the years, but this time it was different. It was one of those "aha" moments in my life and in my growth. It was as if all my pain from betrayals throughout the past thirty years had been touched by these powerful truths of God's Word. That is where change began for me. It was God's Word touching the deepest place of my heart.

Change is possible when our experiences intersect the truth of His word.

That is what we call the cross. It was at the cross that Jesus' earthly story intersected his Father's heavenly story. It was in this "aha" moment that my deepest pain, anger, disappointment, abandonment, rejection and betrayal began to somewhat dissipate. No, they didn't just magically disappear, but for some amazing reason, I was able to see clearly again. I was able to see hope again in the midst of betrayal's fog. You see, I was in one of the darkest seasons I have ever been in as a pastor and a follower of Jesus. I had just experienced another betrayal and was, one more time, deeply wounded. Another long and arduous journey of healing had begun. It was in this moment, as I was reading through the scriptures, that I had what I describe as a very deep emotional and spiritual V8 moment!

Only God can do something like this, but while I was reading Jesus' words, all the emotions and feelings from the betrayal began to calm down within me. Peace did become still in the midst of the turmoil. I'm still not jumping up and down celebrating and eagerly waiting for the next betrayal in my life, but somehow in this moment, these not-so-uplifting words that Jesus spoke really began to lift me up. If he said we will be betrayed, then guess what? There is a good chance we will be betrayed. It was His Word that day that gave me a sense of strength to get through it differently. I realized that the Lord was not shocked by this betrayal. So if He wasn't shocked, and He knew it was going to happen, then that meant He had a way to get me through it. I was confident that He was going to help me get to the other side of it. Maybe you have experienced betrayal and find yourself stuck in the pain, anger and shock. Let me encourage you to trust that although you have a journey of healing ahead of you, Jesus already sees you on the other side of it! Free from the pain. Free from the bitterness, resentment and hatred. Free from all that holds you back from living a full life. Even though it may seem impossible right now, trust that God is with you and try to see yourself as victorious as He does. You won't be able to do this apart from His Word. Trust me, HE is with you! Trust me, HE is for you.

    My prayer is that this book will help you gain Biblical insight and understanding into the insidiousness of betrayal and help you to recognize the signs of destruction that betrayal leaves in its wake. Perhaps even more important is that this book will help those of you who have experienced betrayal to see clearly again and find the hope and strength to move *Beyond Betrayal*. If you have experienced betrayal and feel you are stuck, I want to let you know that it is possible to get back up, dust yourself off and move forward. You can be full of hope in God's plan for your life again. God desires that we won't be ignorant but have understanding. I believe that division through betrayal is one of the devil's major schemes in the days we are living, and it is important that we are not in the dark concerning this issue.

As you continue reading this book, we will look at the three most common types of betrayers, three things they lust for, and the three underlying, unhealthy heart issues that drive betrayers. Finally, I want to answer how to get beyond the pain of our own personal betrayals. You see, betrayal is going to happen and we all feel the effects of it one way or another. After all, Jesus warned us it would happen. If you have been betrayed, you don't have to let it keep you from the abundant life God promises.

You can live victoriously '*Beyond Betrayal*' and be restored to your purpose and passion.

Questions:
What could we do if we stopped the betrayal within our churches? Could we really

reach the world? Could we really advance the kingdom of God in a way that honors Him? Could we really be a part of the Ephesians 3:20 experience?

I'd like to think so, but it's going to take all of us. God has already given us all we need to make the necessary changes. Jesus desires that we would be one and in order for that to happen, we must get *Beyond Betrayal*. Say it with me: No more broken churches.

1. I Love The Church

She has so many different shapes, sizes, styles, expressions, traditions, cultures, and labels, yet all of her forms have been purposed with the same purpose. She has had some great successes and some God-awful and embarrassing failures. Since her beginning, she has been loved-hated, honored-dishonored, exalted-undermined, cherished-battered, empowered-divided, understood-misrepresented, and yet, after all these decades and centuries, she is still breathing and living. She is at the center of God's heart and the target of Satan's attacks. The one thing that keeps her strong and alive through it all is what so many seem to forget along the way - purpose. No other purpose on the planet is greater. The Church's purpose has unlimited potential, and yet many times what we see is that the purpose is often confused, misunderstood and misaligned. Instead of reaching for the high place of the purpose, many times we see her dwelling in the cellar and never reaching that potential. She shows up for the meeting, but can miss the point of that meeting altogether. Throughout the years, she has brought transformation to cities, states and nations, and sadly, she has caused much hurt, confusion and heartache to the people she was purposed for. At times, she seems to have caused more harm than good. Yes, what I am describing is the wonderful thing called the Church.

Yet, with all her successes and failures, the Church is still the primary vehicle God desires to use to change the world.

The Bible tells us that Jesus will eventually present the Church to his Father without spot, wrinkle or blemish.

Sadly, the Church doesn't always act like a bride preparing for that presentation day. In fact, it seems many have forgotten. And yet, through all of our issues, Jesus loves the Church (His bride) greatly and still has great plans for her. The Church still remains the apple of His eye.

After all, I still love her

It is with great gratitude that I can say wholeheartedly that I love the Church. I am not a church basher although I could be, and I would be very good at it. I love the 'Big C' Church, as well as the potential of the 'little C' local church. I love what the Church is called to stand for and whom to stand for. I love what I see when a group of people come together in unity, and great things are done. I love the multiple expressions that are shown within a healthy church. I love being a part of something that is much bigger than me. I love most of the evolution within the Church over the decades and centuries. I find that my love and passion for the Church is still growing, and the expectancy and anticipation is higher than it ever has been. My love for the church comes with no apologies and with no hesitation. Sadly, this has not always been the case, mostly due to the hurtful betrayals and divisions I have experienced in local churches over the years.

The hurtful actions I have seen from pastors, people in leadership, and seasoned veterans in the church world have caused me, at times, to not be so proud. Actually, some of my experiences over the years have led to much embarrassment and shame for the Church. There was a short season I didn't even want to admit I was a part of a particular church that once flourished for the kingdom. That's pretty sad. I have often wondered how something that was meant to be so beautiful, radiant and powerful could become so ugly, mean and weak. A church that at one time was doing great things for God whose members appeared to love each other greatly, now couldn't seem to get along for anything. How could there be so much betrayal, division and hurt within the Church? Should the church really be experiencing this? The answer is no, but sadly it did, and it does. But as much as I was once embarrassed by the local church, I am now much more passionate about seeing it successful and alive. There were a few times I had my doubts in the church and was tempted to disengage, but there was something, or I guess "someone," that would not let me.

My Church Life

My whole life has been involved with the church in some form or another. Since birth, I have been a part of church. In fact, when I was little, the story is that I had fallen asleep on a pew during service. Must've been an amazing message! Apparently as my parents were driving away from the church, they realized they had forgotten something...ME! They left me sleeping...on the pew. That is hilarious. Don't worry, after years of counseling...I think I'm now over it!

Anyhow, whether it has been attending, serving, visiting, traveling in ministry, being a youth pastor or worship leader and now serving as a lead pastor, I have been there. Call me nuts, but I even like visiting other churches when I'm on vacation. Even in my early college years when I was somewhat disconnected from the Lord, I would still find myself in the church doing something. Hats off to my parents for a job well done. In my early years, we were raised in a Baptist denomination and then, for an extended season, we transitioned to a Pentecostal church. We were so creative that we adopted the name "bapticostals." When I graduated high school, I connected with some people from an Assembly of God church. After a few years there, I began attending a predominantly white non- denominational church and then transferred to a predominantly black non- denominational church. I also spent some time in a Catholic church for a season. Now I currently pastor a great church with some of the greatest people in the world. One thing is for certain, even though the denominations and names on the signs were all different, the people issues were still the same. The issues of betrayal within the church are not about a denomination, race or style of church. I believe betrayal happens in our churches because people fall asleep in the pew, ultimately forgetting the original "purpose" for why we are called together.

The Good and the Bad

Throughout all these years, I have seen some crazy things in the church world. I have seen God use a church in amazing ways. I have seen people saved, healed and delivered. I have seen some local churches grow exponentially and sadly, I have seen many churches close their doors. I have seen vibrant churches of over a thousand people betray, divide and destroy something awesome. I have seen many churches do a wonderful job fulfilling the intended purpose for which they were called while on the other hand, I have seen other churches lose sight of that purpose…or maybe they never had it to begin with. I have seen some powerful moves of God in churches, while at the same time watched some of them destroy that very move of God. You don't have to look too far to find yet another story of another church who has lost their way. I am amazed at the amount of betrayal and hurt that has happened and still happens within churches. Going back to our opening scriptures; betrayal will come from parents, brethren, kinfolks and friends.

"many will fall away and betray one another and hate one another"
- Matthew 24:10

When we read about the early days of the church in Acts, there were some great things that were accomplished. Many people were saved, baptized, set free, fed, clothed and raised to a place of leadership. Overall, the early church grew, but there were also some issues they had that have remained common throughout the centuries regardless of the size of church, denomination, city, color and culture. They are the issues and problems that have caused the church to not look so good and appetizing to the communities and world to which they are called. The divisions, fights, sins and betrayals that have caused so many to wander around spiritually with wounded faith, eroded trust, and confusion often find themselves living life disconnected from the church. So maybe we should stand back and take an honest look and ask ourselves "Why would the world want to be part of this?"

A friend of mine, Bob, shared with me a story about their former church from back in the 90's. It was a vibrant and growing church where over eleven hundred people would show up weekly. This church was on fire! The praise and worship was alive and anointed. The pastor was a very dynamic preacher with a great teaching gift, and Bob attributed much of his spiritual growth and development to him. His pastor's influence around the nation was rapidly growing, and God was using him in great ways. The buy-in from the people was at an all-time high, and it felt as if his church was on its way to do some great things for the kingdom. This pastor was great at communicating the vision, and this church appeared to be unstoppable! Then one day it all fell apart. It was as if a grenade went off and within months his former church completely unraveled. The senior pastor was caught lying, misusing the finances and having an affair with someone in the church. In addition, there were several affairs that were happening from other church leadership within the church. When all this was exposed, the whole thing crumbled. Sadly, his former church is no longer in existence. Still today, when I talk with him or others that were members there, they bring up the pain of what took place way back then. His words still stick with me after all these years when he told me "we feel betrayed." For some the pain is still fresh even though the betrayal was years ago.

Now you may be thinking, "This happens everywhere," and I would agree with you. That is what makes it so difficult. The number of people whose hearts and faith are wounded by some form of betrayal in the church is way too high. These people in Bob's former church trusted their leaders, bought into the vision and invested their lives, prayers and resources into it. It's sad to see the number of people who have been wounded and feel betrayed by their leadership. Many of the people from Bob's former church are still wandering from church to church, not attending anywhere at all, or are part-timers. Some are still afraid to plant roots and afraid to re-engage at that level again. Some may even attend another church, but their involvement hasn't been the same. The bottom line is that leadership betrayal is devastating and leads to many broken people. There are a number of stories like this across the nation that have caused a lack of trust in people today.

I would love to be able to say betrayal in the church is not the case, but I can't. What I can say is that betrayal will continue to exist in the church because people exist in the church. Yes, these will even be the ones who have been saved, redeemed, gifted, anointed and called by God to reach people.

God Wants Healthy Churches

God has many great churches, both small and large (in numbers), that are doing powerful things in advancing his kingdom.

I don't believe that God looks nor cares about the sign out front or denomination. His issue is whether we have the love of Jesus expressed in our churches. He's looking for unity, people that are focused on reaching the lost, and a church that practices the character and heart of Christ. God will move in any denomination and any local church in a great way simply because they are moving together in a healthy way and possessing right hearts. The healthiness to which I am referring involves unity, serving together, honoring each other, submitting to his delegated leaders, and displaying character and integrity. These seem to be the most common characteristics of healthy churches. It's not about the membership size or the denomination, but the healthiness of the culture within the local church.

Years ago, I heard a preacher say that "the church is the greatest hope for the world." I fell in love with that quote the day I heard it, and I agree wholeheartedly with it.

In no disrespect to his statement, I believe that a 'healthy' church is the greatest hope for the world.

Sadly, there are many churches on our street corners that are no hope to the world. They are just a building with people who meet in it. They may have the hope of the world (Jesus), but refuse to get out and be that hope. In fact, there are many churches that simply refuse to stay together and get along. When you walk into their churches, the environment alone says you aren't welcome. The name on their sign and building structure have done nothing more than create a barrier between the hope and the people who need to know this hope. There are many things that some churches have done that have not helped the Church's case overall in being the greatest hope for the world. Thankfully, there are thousands of churches that have, and these are the ones who are moving forward to create healthy churches! For this reason, people are attending these places.

Why I love her?

My love for the Church today is not because all my experiences have been great, or because the church is perfect or fully healthy. It's not because I am a pastor. In fact, if it weren't for God's healing me, I would still be angry and may have walked away. You see, while I was in my greatest disappointments, pain and anger from the back-stabbings and betrayals, God grabbed hold of my heart, and He helped me turn my anger and shame into a hope and love for his church - not just the one I pastor, but all of the big 'C' Church. I had realized in that dark season just how much He deeply loves me and how much He loves people and I was able to begin the journey of forgiveness toward others. It was in this season my heart began to expand greatly for others and the church. Now my love for the church today is based solely on the intense love that Jesus has for His bride, even with all her issues. I love that I'm a part of something that Jesus is for and not against.

I believe wholeheartedly in the calling, purpose and plan that God has given his church. I love that God still uses the Church to reach people who are distant from him. I love that God hasn't given up on the Church. I believe that fulfilling God's purposes is done through healthy churches who will stay true to their calling. I am passionate about being a pastor that helps create healthy environments, healthy churches, healthy people and healthy families. I do believe it's possible to be the church we are called to be. However, the focus must go from just 'doing' the church thing to 'being' the church. We cannot be the church while we are disconnected from one other. We must make a decision together that we will have no more broken churches. While it is in our power to do so, lets do it! The world is waiting.

As you continue reading, I pray that these insights will help you to get 'Beyond Betrayal' and to engage fully in the hope and calling that God has given you. Maybe you have been disappointed and ashamed by the actions of a local church. Today can be the day your love for the church can be restored to a place you never dreamed. Together we can make a shift in the church world for generations to come.

Say it with me... "NO MORE BROKEN CHURCHES!".

2. Who Are They?

The Many Faces of Betrayers

In order for us to get 'Beyond Betrayal' and have 'No More Broken Churches,' we must get a greater understanding of this concept of betrayal. To lessen and even stop it in our churches, we must first understand how it operates, what to watch for and how to protect ourselves from becoming the betrayer. Read again what Jesus says about betrayal.

You will be betrayed even by parents, brothers and sisters, relatives and friends, and they will put some of you to death.
- Luke 21:16 (NIV)

Notice the list of betrayers that Jesus gives us in the above scriptures. It's pretty sobering when we see the list and who the people represent in our lives. They are moms, dads, sisters, brothers, friends, pastors, ministry or business partners, coaches and/or leaders. The list Jesus gives us represents so many people. The thing to notice is they are people who are very close to us, people whom we love dearly, and who say they love(d) us and people we have lived with and shared the most intimate times. Betrayers will be people who know what you laugh at and what causes you tears. These betrayers may know your passions, and they may know your strengths and weaknesses. (Some know what your favorites are regarding many things.) They are possibly on your top five favorites on the iPhone... or Android (if that's how you roll). They are the ones that will be on your speed dial. They are not all your 'so-called' friends on Facebook– give me a break! They are your real friends in this journey of life. They are people who are on the inside. They are the ones you have trusted, confided in, and opened up your life (heart) to. They are the ones who are 'in-the-know' of your life. These people know you. They have inside information on your life. You may have spent years with them. The truth is, betrayers are close.

• It's the business partner that is with you in the planning room building the dream, but working behind your back to take it away from you.

• It's the person at church or in business that you have poured your heart and soul into that you find out later is spreading lies, rumors and is undermining you. Their sole purpose is getting you removed from position because they want what you have.

• It's that pastor or leader that you have submitted to. You believed them, trusted them, given finances and time to their vision...only to watch them leave. They talked big plans, but walked away with little or no follow through.

You thought they would never walk away... but did.

• It's that friend with whom you have the serious, heart-revealing conversations who then chooses to use the information against you.

• It's that parent or spouse that walks out the door never to return.

• It's the staff member that puts up a front that they are totally with you in the meetings, and yet is divisively spreading lies and undermining you behind your back.

• It's the spouse that comes home from work every day and gives that kiss on the cheek, while kissing someone else at work on the other cheek. (That's not what Jesus meant in Matt 5:39 when he said to turn the other cheek.)

• It's the close friend that says repeatedly "I'm with you," and you find out it was all a lie.

What's my point?

Betrayal doesn't happen with strangers.

Strangers can say a lot of things about you, but you will work through that fairly quickly. Strangers or outsiders are ignorant. What do they know? Their words don't carry the same weight as those from people who are close to you. When people that don't know me talk about me, I don't feel betrayed by them. I just know that they don't have a clue, but when people who know my heart betray...it hurts badly and, depending on who the betrayer is, can sometimes take years to heal.

Maybe you're in the midst of a betrayal right now. Maybe it is a spouse through an affair. Maybe you have been betrayed by a leader, a pastor or some kind of mentor in your life. Maybe you were promised something and were passed over. Maybe the betrayal was simply the promise that a certain someone would be there and they up and left you. Maybe you found out that a very close friend has been spreading lies behind your back. It could be a number of things. It really doesn't matter what the story is - betrayal is painful and it hurts! My belief is that betrayal is the most painful thing we can go through as people.

Dr Bob Nichols, a friend who has a PHD in psychology, states that "rejection, abandonment and betrayal are the three most hurtful wounds in people's lives." After the things I have dealt with in my life and with over twenty years of helping others work through issues in their own lives - I know his statement is right on. I've often wondered if betrayal is the reason why so many people live with rejection and abandonment issues. Could betrayal be the key that opens the door for abandonment and rejection? Either way, betrayal is a problem we must deal with. We have a younger generation who knows a lot about betrayal, and we are seeing the ramifications. They are displaying the effects of their betrayal at a rapid rate. Many are afraid to commit relationally and are unable to understand the value of relationships. Many are wanting the benefits of marriage without having to fully commit to it. Betrayal has become the reason why many marriages begin with pre- nuptial agreements. How sad is it that so many marriages begin with a lack of trust and an underlying expectation of separation?

What is Betrayal?

Betrayal is the act of misleading someone and using deception to get something we want. It breeds unfaithfulness in relationships and disappointment from unrealistic expectations of others. When I think of betrayers, I have to mention the word "pretender." After all, this is what they are. They are skilled at putting up fronts, but then move out and attack. Betrayers are purposeful at working behind someone's back for personal gain. Typically, betrayal will blindside and knock the wind out of our sails. A betrayer's actions are similar to pulling the carpet out from underneath us, and can even derail us from our destiny if we let them. My wife has said that "betrayal is much like a dagger to the back or a blunt force blow to the heart." It can be as deadly as an arrow, surprising as a dagger or as deceptive as a simple kiss on the cheek. In the Bible, King Saul threw an arrow at David from across the room. Absalom took a dagger (figuratively) and stabbed His father in the back. Judas kissed Jesus on the cheek. No matter how betrayal comes at you, it's painful.

Betrayal happens on purpose and is always a premeditated plan. I don't like using the word "always," but it is appropriate. Betrayal is purposeful and intentional. It never happens by accident. No one ever *just* undermines and divides. No one ever *just* has an affair. No one ever *just* steps up and splits a church. Betrayers premeditate and know exactly where to hit you.

Remember, betrayers are the ones who are close to you. Over time, betrayal grows from a small seed within, and when the time is right, the betrayer will act. Betrayers are gifted at justifying their actions and will never call what they have done "betrayal." In the church world, people may call it "listening to God's voice;" however what we see is that their action is divisive and evil in nature. The betrayer's goal is to knock someone down or take someone out to get what they want.

What does the betrayer want?

There are three goals or focuses a betrayer could have: possessions, power and/or position. The goal(s) will be at least one or all three of these reasons, and the pursuit of these goals is driven by a lust within to gain something the betrayer feels will satisfy. Barring a move of God toward repentance, once betrayers launch their efforts toward their goal, there is no turning back for them. The reason is that they become entwined in a web of lies, deceit and self-justification. Although these lies and deception may start small, they grow into full-blown betrayal which manifests from unhealthy heart issues, personal (competing) agendas, selfish ambitions and control issues. I'll cover all of these in more detail later.

Betrayal Started Here

Throughout history, when betrayal happened, the betrayers were killed for their actions. People were hung in public, decapitated and openly punished. Sadly in our day, it is now a glorified action. Betrayal sells. It makes for interesting movies, TV series and tabloids. We see betrayal so much now in real life issues and in Hollywood that it almost appears to be a normal way of life. According to Jesus, betrayal will continue to happen and is here to stay. The truth is that as long as people and the betrayer of all still exists (the devil), there will always be the possibility and opportunity for betrayals. We are all susceptible to becoming the betrayer as well as being victims of betrayal. Hey, if Satan (Lucifer) was able to influence one-third of the angels - who were in the presence of God 24/7 - into betraying God, then all of us are open to this action. Read Isaiah 14:12-17, Ezekiel 28:16, Revelation 12:4,7-9.

Lucifer and the fallen angels birthed the very first betrayal, and it was a big one in that a third of heaven emptied out because of it. Then betrayal happened again in Genesis with Adam and Eve and it grew like wild fire after that. The Bible is full of stories of betrayal and in turn, thousands of stories of betrayal throughout history have shown that we as people are susceptible to the betrayal. Even with all the history and all the stories of betrayal, I still remain hopeful that we, as God's people, can stop or lessen the betrayal within the church and keep from having more broken churches. I happen to believe that we have the power as followers of Jesus to do this not only within the church, but also within our homes and in our own worlds. It will take a healthy people to do this. It will take healthy leadership, healthy pastors, healthy parents, healthy people, healthy teams, healthy families, honesty, humility and hard work. Notice the key word, though? Healthy.

As you read forward, I will be exposing some of the key characteristics, motives and actions of people who betray. Throughout the chapters, my references mostly cover betrayal within the Church, but these truths and insights can be applied to leaders, businesses, families, and relationships...well, pretty much anywhere people that are supposed to work together exist.

My hope is that as you read this, you will

gain a better understanding as to how betrayers operate, their motivations and focuses that pull the strings in their betrayal. Just know that even with a greater knowledge of betrayers, very seldom will you see betrayal coming. That fact of life is what makes betrayal so painful and agonizing. Unfortunately, in order to gain a full understanding of betrayal, knowledge and experience are needed, and even with knowledge and experience, you still won't be able to fully keep yourself from betrayal. That is, unless you become a hermit and completely disconnect from people. I guess this is an option, but I assure you, it's not God's best for you.

3. Absalom-Style Betrayers

There are three primary betrayers that I want to shed a little light on from the Bible. They are from different times in history, but their lives, actions and stories still end with the same result, betrayal which leads to death. The common result with betrayal is DEATH - the betrayer's own physical death, the death of the people around him or her or even sometimes both. Although we don't see betrayal leading to physical death so much today, we do see betrayal leading to death in many other areas of our lives. We see death in relationships, churches, families, businesses, hope, trust, passions, callings, dreams, ministries and even the death of someone's personal faith.

When it comes to dealing with betrayers, not everything is as it appears because they are usually great pretenders. In this first story of betrayal, we learn of a man who is so skilled in the art of betrayal, he is able to lure hundreds of people to follow him. This man, Absalom, was skilled at pretending and consequently deceived many. He was motivated for his own personal gain and he had a goal he was determined to accomplish. What was his goal? - to get a position and to gain the power he wanted at any cost.

Back story: Absalom's father was King

David and his mother was Maakah (2 Samuel 3:3). Absalom's relationship with his father was strained to say the least, and he eventually betrayed King David and his kingdom. He conspired behind King David's back to win the people over to himself and even tried to steal his kingdom from him.

The Absalom-style betrayer gives us nine characteristics and actions from which we can learn.

1. Don't be fooled

The bible points out something interesting - Absalom's outward appearance. Apparently, he was good looking, and we need to know that he was the best looking man in the land. This makes me laugh a bit. Of all the stuff to write about Absalom, we get to read about his good looks. The Bible also lets us know that he had some serious hair and a good size family.

In all Israel there was not a man so highly praised for his handsome appearance as Absalom. From the top of his head to the sole of his foot there was no blemish in him. 26 Whenever he cut the hair of his head—he used to cut his hair once a year because it became too heavy for him—he would weigh it, and its weight was two hundred shekels by the royal standard.
- 2 Samuel 14:25

C'mon now! This man was actually praised for his good looks? And no blemishes? What's up with that? Not sure that many of us could use the 'no-blemish' card. I know I can't. Most of us could find several blemishes right now. And what's up with the hair? 200 shekels? That's approximately five pounds! That's some serious hair! The funny thing is that a lot of men had long hair in the Bible, and I don't recall many of them being mentioned for their hair except for the bald guy and the kids who were killed because they jeered at him! (If you take a look at my picture, you will see that three pounds of hair a year wasn't in the cards for my life.) Anyhow, Absalom was put together pretty well. The brother had it going on. Men wanted to be him, women wanted to be with him, and if his having all the looks wasn't enough, the Bible says his kids were good looking too. Must have been some good genetics. My guess is that if he lived in our day, he would probably have his own reality show. Maybe instead of the Kardashians, it would be the Absalom family. It's interesting that the Bible doesn't mention much of his character, his heart after God or love for people, but we do see his true character through his actions.

I believe the Bible makes mention of his outward appearance for great reasons - to show us that you can have the outward appearance, but who you are on the inside is what really matters.

> In his physical appearance, Absalom had it going on, but what he really was (on the inside) is what people eventually saw.

We all know that our exterior changes...we wrinkle, sag, get a little larger around the mid section; we get shorter, the hair thins out a bit... or even falls out. Our once bulging biceps turn into sagging triceps. Our once six pack abs turns into the kegger and can conveniently be used to hold a plate of food while sitting on the couch. Now depending on your age, you're either saying with confidence "not gonna happen to me" or you are in the midst of some of these changes right now and are giving me the silent "amen!"

Many times in leadership, it is easy to focus on the outward and not what really matters. Immature, needy, and especially inexperienced leaders get caught up in this. Ever had someone on your team that talked the part? They knew the leadership terms, scriptures, worship songs, taught classes and carried passion to do the job. They looked good and appeared to be authentic, but over time their true colors began to shine through. The selfishness, control issues, competition with other co-leaders, need for attention, insecurities, jealousy, dishonesty and more began to surface. You didn't see it early on because it typically takes time for the "real person" to show up. Just like Absalom, a person's true nature will eventually be revealed. The stuff inside the heart can no longer be hidden behind the mask of a gift, ability or outward image. Someone may have a great gifting, or may be able to sing or teach (exterior), but they lack the character, integrity, people skills, teachability, and humility (interior) that is needed to make it long term. Absalom-style betrayers know how to look the part and can fake it for a long time, but lingering inside their hearts are those issues that if not dealt with, often will result in betrayal and division.

Leaders need to be careful not to keep a person in position solely on their gifting or skill set. These qualities may get them in the door initially, but their healthy interior (character, integrity, humility, teachability, fruit of the Spirit (Gal 5:22-23), and more), allows them to stay in the house. A person may be hired or placed in position because of gifting, but allowing him or her to remain there while displaying a pattern of unhealthiness can be very damaging to the people surrounding that person and to your vision. All too often we see this trend in the church because the needs are so great. Someone may have a gifting you need as a leader, but their actions will eventually fight the flow of the vision and team. This was the case with Absalom. He had something seriously wrong on the inside.

Yes, God looks at the heart of people, but we don't always get to see the heart...until later on down the road. When God selected David to be the next king of Israel to replace Saul, he wasn't selected because of his outward features and talents. In fact, his brothers were better looking and even physically stronger. God selected David because of his heart. He loved the personal connection, and his willingness to serve, love and honor. He loved his warrior strength and the worshipper he was. God's selection process doesn't always make sense. What matters most to God is our hearts. I remember my mom telling me early on in ministry that "God doesn't call the qualified, but he always qualifies the called." He focuses on the heart first and then helps you build the skill sets to accomplish something great with your life. No amount of good looks and gifting can make up for poor character issues. Don't be fooled into keeping someone in position because of their gifting alone. Absalom-style betrayers lust for position and power and will place the focus of their attention on how they look in front of people.

Now let's go a little deeper into the heart and actions of an Absalom-style betrayer.

In the course of time, Absalom provided himself with a chariot and horses and with fifty men to run ahead of him. He would get up early and stand by the side

of the road leading to the city gate. Whenever anyone came with a complaint to be placed before the king for a decision, Absalom would call out to him, "What town are you from?" He would answer, "Your servant is from one of the tribes of Israel." Then Absalom would say to him, "Look, your claims are valid and proper, but there is no representative of the king to hear you." And Absalom would add, "If only I were appointed judge in the land! Then everyone who has a complaint or case could come to me and I would see that they receive justice." Also, whenever anyone approached him to bow down before him, Absalom would reach out his hand, take hold of him and kiss him. Absalom behaved in this way toward all the Israelites who came to the king asking for justice, and so he stole the hearts of the people of Israel.
- 2 Samuel 15:1-6 (NIV)

2. Self-Provider - I'll do it myself.

One of the first things we see is that Absalom provided himself with a chariot and horses and with fifty men to run ahead of him.

Question - Why did he have to provide for himself the chariots, horses and men to create this image? The answer is because he wasn't a legit leader and therefore had to create for himself an image that he had a position and had legitimate power.

> When someone feels illegitimate, their tendency is to work harder to prove their legitimacy

This statement is especially true of people who are in a place of leadership. They dress up the outward in order for others to not see who they really are.

Remember: Betrayers are after power, position and/or possessions, and when people have to create these for themselves, they have to do a lot more work to appear legitimate. Years ago, we had a young leader coming up in the ministry who had a track record of sharing exaggerated ministry stories, so as to paint the picture that this person was a legit leader. This person's stories and striving to paint an image made me feel as if I were sitting next to Billy Graham. What's crazy is that the closer we came to seeing who this person really was, the greater and more intense the stories became. Sadly, this person is no longer in the ministry today and could never get this area of legitimacy settled within. This person created a fake image for others to see, which resulted in his living the lie(s) which could only be sustained by his own self-effort. Absalom did the same thing.

Absalom-style betrayers create false images of their position and power and will do whatever is needed to make it appear legit. Absalom had to establish his lies by creating the appearance that he had position and power. He knew how to play the role and look the part, and he knew what the people looked for in a leader. After all, he was part of the royal family. Remember, Absalom was King David's son. The crazy thing here is that he could've eventually inherited all the position and power that he ever dreamed of. Unfortunately, Absalom wasn't willing to wait for that day. He wasn't a legit leader and he wasn't willing to settle the issues inside his heart; therefore he had to "provide for himself" the position and power so that others would follow him. Sadly, I have seen support pastors or key leaders in the church who created their own place of position and/or power in ministry. Many have even been given a delegated position, but because of their personal drive for higher position, more power or some kind of possession, they stepped out and had to "provide for themselves."

Self-providers run ahead of God's timing and blessing.

Self-providers take the influence and authority - given by God through the leadership - and step out of their sphere of authority. Some are discontent with where they are in ministry (or life) and feel they should be further down the road. Some are frustrated with God and/or their leaders' timing. Some want the position of a senior pastor so badly that they will leave the church they are serving and start one right down the road. They seductively use their influence to take as many people with them as possible, all along feeling they were doing the will of God. But when someone has to "provide for themselves" by creating their own position and power, it's either not the right timing or not the right thing. I'm not talking of church planters who are sent and called to do so. I'm speaking of the ones who undermine and betray their senior pastor, their leaders and the people with whom they are serving.

The danger is in starting something that is not God's plan. In the church world, we call that an Ishmael. This term is used when something created out of self-effort, and serves as a substitution for God's intended plan. It's man's feeble attempt at forcing something to come to pass, and then slapping God's name on it. In Genesis, God made a promise to Abraham and his wife that they were going to have a son. After years of waiting and I'm sure after much trying, the result was no baby! They became impatient, as most of us would and Sarah has this great idea. She told Abraham to go and sleep with her maid (Hagar) and make a baby. That is bizarre to me! So, of course, he obeys his wife and Ishmael was born. What do we see here? We see Abraham and Sarah getting out in front of God and having to self-provide for the promise. Why? Because they felt they had waited too long. After all, in their eyes God was late. My point here is that Ishmael was not the promised son, but a forced substitution for the promise. God's original plan was to bless Abraham and Sarah, not Abraham and Hagar. God wanted Isaac as the promise, not Ishmael.

One similarity to Absalom is that Abraham and Sarah self-provided for their blessing; they were motivated by their own agendas. Most of us wouldn't think of Abraham and Sarah as betrayers, but that is exactly what they were. Sarah ended up hating Hagar who had faithfully served her and Abraham, and they sent both Hagar and Ishmael away to go live somewhere else. How messed up is that? Hagar was just serving away and one day here comes Abraham saying "Lets make a baby!" So Ishmael was born and then, Abraham and Sarah betray them both and sent them away.

More times than not, betrayers don't start out with the intent to betray. Many of them are good people. Although they're not evil, they do become deceived, and their deception can cause them to do some evil and hurtful things. Their lust for position, power or possession opens the door for them to act out in betrayal. This is what Abraham and Absalom did. This is what people in ministry do. They move ahead of God's timing and their leaders' blessing and self-provide for their own thing. Still to this day, I have not seen a church, ministry or person who went out and provided his own way and had any kind of long-term success. Most of the churches I know that began with forcing the issue like this all closed their doors within a couple of years - some within months. Several of the ministers have either fallen in sin, given up, or are ministering to same 25 people with whom they left 25 years ago. Why? Because when God births a church or ministry, it lasts and it grows! It will last through the darkest of times and through the worst of adversity, and the gates of hell will not be able to overcome it. When we have to force a promise of God out of frustration, impatience or rebellion, we will have to provide for ourselves just like Absalom did. God's blessing cannot and will not fully be on it. When God gives you a vision or promise, forcing it to happen can be extremely dangerous and will produce a lot of unnecessary heartaches - for you and others. If God has called you, just stay the course, stay submitted, and stay obedient. If it's God idea, it will come to pass. Just remain faithful to what he has for you now.

3. The Private Meetings

Another characteristic of betrayers is that they love to have the private meetings.

"He would get up early and stand by the side of the road leading to the city gate."

Notice in the above passage how Absalom woke up early so he could get out to the "side of the road" that leads to the city gate. Question - If Absalom was truly a king's representative, and if he was truly operating in his proper authority, why would he have to go outside the city gate and meet with the people on the "side of the road?" Why the private (side-road) meetings? The answer is that hee wasn't a legitimate king's representative; therefore he had to create the look that he was one. If the conversations had been held out in public, Absalom would have been exposed.

Important to know: Ancient kings were more than the heads of government, they were also the "supreme court" of their kingdom. If someone believed that a local court did not give him justice he appealed to the court of the king where the king or a representative of the king heard his case.

A real representative of the king wouldn't set up these private meetings on a side of the road. A king's representative would hear the people inside the city or at the palace - not in secret. Absalom set up on the roadside because he didn't want to be seen or found out. He operated outside his authority. He bypassed the way the kingdom was set up because he thought he knew better and he was hungry for power.

Absalom-style betrayers never work alone. They need a following, and the greater the following, the greater the power. When talking to a friend who serves as a pastor, he was sharing with me about an issue of betrayal from a staff member in his church. This betrayer was much like Absalom. When his betrayal finally did come to light, my friend found a trail of "side of the road" meetings with others in the church. The betrayal may have hit him suddenly, but when the story unfolded, he found that it really had been in the works for quite a while. It was just underground in the inner workings of the heart and behind closed doors. The truth is: betrayal is a premeditated act that germinates in the side-road (private) conversations. Betrayers won't call it betrayal because they are so caught in their web of lies and deceit, they will place a more spiritual label on it and give it an appearance of God.

Years ago, we had a high level staff member at the church who pulled me aside in his office and proceeded to tell me that it was time for me to take over the reigns of the church. Basically, in a 'private, side-road' meeting, he was asking me to "provide for myself" the position of Senior Pastor. Although he seemed sincere for the well being of the church and mine, I felt his conversation was that "private, side-of-the-road" meeting where betrayers do their work. I was not the senior pastor at this time, but it was becoming more apparent that this was the direction the church was headed. This kind of conversation happened twice with two different leaders who obviously had prior "private, side-road" conversations among themselves. I wasn't stupid...I turned my palms up and said, "I don't have to take or force anything." I will only receive what is given to me. I wasn't about to be an Absalom. Plus, the leadership of the church wasn't mine to take, and I wasn't in a hurry. If it is God, you don't have to force it, take it or cheat for it.

Remember: If it's God's idea, it will happen in His timing and His way.

It is my opinion and experience that many people who betray don't begin with betrayal in mind, but because of the unhealthy areas of their hearts, eventually the unhealthiness begins to lead their actions.

The Bible gives us a clear picture as to what happens inside the heart of a betrayer.

But each person is tempted when they are dragged away by their own evil desire and enticed. Then, after desire has conceived, it gives birth to sin; and sin, when it is full-grown, gives birth to death.
- James 1:14-15 (NIV)

We all are tempted with the same temptations. The only difference between people who betray and people who don't is that betrayers allow their evil desire to conceive and open the door for the act of betrayal. This person's lust for power, possessions and/or position has been conceived in their heart, and this lust births sin and death.

Every betrayer at some point has a moment of decision as to whether to move forward in betrayal or not.

After one of our former pastors left the church, we had to do some cleanup. We talked with some members of our church, and we were blown away by the number of 'side-road' conversations about the leadership and other co-leaders. We couldn't believe the number of lies, misleading comments, and private meetings that were held by this person. It became quite apparent that this trail of lies and deceit we stumbled on led to the act of betrayal. When a person's betrayal goes public, don't be surprised. Chances are, you may find a trail of private meetings and conversations that will typically lead back months and maybe even longer. What may have started out as a simple discussion became private, "side-road" meetings, resulting in patterns of discussions, complaints and concerns about other areas of the church and eventually undermining the delegated leader(s) and overall vision. This person covertly inflates himself by belittling others. I'm convinced that once the seed of betrayal takes root inside someone, barring a miracle from God - his plan will be executed.

Absalom-style betrayers usually begin with one or two key people with whom they are close. Betrayers will cross the lines of their delegated influence to gain more of a following and increase their own influence. The conversations they have with others slowly turn to issues that they have no responsibility to change.

For instance, a leader who is over the cafe area begins handling concerns and complaints about the production team leaders. Instead of sending the people to the proper oversight of that department, he listens to the people as Absalom did. The goal of Absalom-style betrayers is to win the people's hearts. They need a following. With an Absalom-style betrayer, the betrayal is only as powerful as his following, and these kinds of betrayers know it. So they work very hard at winning people to themselves. They are very good at looking the part and creating "side-road" discussions.

4. Having the inside information

Look at what Absalom told the people who came to him.

Whenever anyone came with a complaint to be placed before the king for a decision, Absalom would call out to him, "What town are you from?" He would answer, "Your servant is from one of the tribes of Israel." Then Absalom would say to him, "Look, your claims are valid and proper, but there is no

representative of the king to hear you.".
- 2 Samuel 15:2-3 (NIV)

Absalom-style betrayers love information. In fact, they thrive on it. They want to and need to be "in the know." One of the problems we faced in our church with this style of betrayer was the insatiable hunger for information he had no business knowing. Another common issue we experienced was former leaders' displaying a pattern of knowing the complaints of all the people. We would hear about these complaints regularly at our leadership meetings, and they seemed to always have a handle on the people's complaints. They had the inside information on a lot of issues, and much of it was from outside their sphere of influence and authority. They were the ones that people went to with complaints, because they knew they would be heard.

At first it may not seem like a big deal, but when this pattern emerges, it should raise a red flag. It can appear very pastoral, and one could make the argument that this is what pastors should do. My argument here is that Absalom was looking like a caring leader by hearing the complaints of the people...but his whole goal was to win the hearts of the people because he needed a following. After all, "Leadership wasn't doing it right in their eyes." Absalom-style betrayers live by the motto "Win their heart- win their hand." Remember that the goal for any betrayer is a higher position, power and/or possession, and they need influence to succeed.

Note: Staff members or key leaders who have a pattern of always hearing and bringing the complaints of the people outside their area of influence need to be confronted. I'm talking about a pattern here, not just one time occurrence.

Years ago, when I was serving as a youth pastor and associate pastor, people knew not to come to me with complaints because I would set them straight, or I would make sure they connected with the right person in charge of that area. Our staff and leaders live by certain rules, and when we live them out, people stop coming to stir stuff up. Let me just say that the people in the church should be able to approach leadership with a concern, but when it is not handled correctly, problems happen.

5. Subtle Lies

Absalom-style betrayers are tricky and slippery, they are great with their words. Absalom answered the people correctly in that there "was" no representative "right there" at the "side of the road." Question: Why would there be? That's a random place to meet! We know that a true representative of the king wouldn't meet there. They would meet at the palace, not on the side of the road outside the gate. The truth was that there was a real representative that would hear the claims of the people, but he was in the city operating where and how he was supposed to be. The system was already set up for the people. Absalom's lie here was deceptive and subtle. What we see is that Absalom used a half-truth covered with a caring and sympathetic tone that drew the hearts of the people to himself. You can hear it in his words.

"Look, your claims are valid and proper, but there is no representative of the king to hear you."

He even uses a little empathy here stating that *"they aren't here for you...but I am."* Or *"they don't care for you like I do."*

Absalom-style betrayers will have trails of misleading, half-truths like this. As we worked through one of our past betrayals, we uncovered many half-truths and sometimes even some outright crazy lies. Absalom-style betrayers are very good at twisting and manipulating their words. They are smooth talkers. These betrayers say just enough in their "side-road" meetings to cover their butts in case they ever get back to leadership. When their confronted, the usual response is "I didn't say that" or "that's not what I meant," or "they heard me wrong." Because you were not in the "private, side-road" meeting(s), it's difficult to nail down the truth, and as leaders, we always want to believe the best about the people on our team. So the only thing that we can do is to watch for patterns and confront when needed.

The deception of Absalom-style betrayers is to believe that they have the heart of the people more than the actual leader does. This ground is dangerous because *"all leadership is given by God."* (Rom 13:1) The real danger is when they begin to believe that they can do it a little better than their leader. They may not be shouting it from the mountaintops, but that belief will manifest in those "private, side-road" meetings. It's the slow drip of poison inside their hearts that eventually will poison others. Like Absalom, they will use some empathy and sympathy - giving that understanding nod that says "I see what you see." Absalom said, *"Look, your claims are valid and proper."* Now think about it, these weren't even his claims to validate, but Absalom's empathy increased his followership. If only he could show the care and concern for the people, they would follow him. Absalom-style betrayers will hear the complaints and concerns of the people as a leader should, but through the nodding of the head, sighs, or simple comments such as "I have seen that too," seeds of agreement and contempt begin to germinate the undermining and potential betrayal. Absalom was skilled at projecting a "man of the people" image, but his motive was all for his own personal gain. Absalom- style betrayers in the church function the same way.

6. Attention Getting

"Whenever anyone came with a complaint to be placed before the king for a decision, Absalom would call out to him,"

Notice the passage above reads that when the people were coming with a complaint for the king, Absalom "called out to them" and had to get their attention. When you have to self-provide your own look of position and power, you have to work extra hard at getting people to notice you. Ever met a leader who needed to have so much attention? Well, Absalom-style betrayers are like that. They *want* attention. They *need* attention. They *starve* for attention. They are *addicted* to it. On those occasions when they get the attention, they can play two extremes. Either they display false humility or the attention they receive just isn't enough. It just didn't scratch the itch. Someone who has a drive for attention will never be settled within, no matter the amount. Absalom had to get the people's attention because they didn't even know he was anyone of importance. He was on a "side of the road" outside the city gate. Again, I just want to state that someone who has legitimate position and power by God and leadership doesn't have to go around clamoring for the attention of people. Absalom had to call out to the people because he didn't have legitimate position or power. Remember, he already had to "provide for himself" the look of power and position and then work to get the people's attention.

During one of our clean up seasons of a betrayer, we found a sheet of paper that listed, in great detail, the responsibilities for their department, which at first glance seemed harmless, but it also listed all the other pastors and a fraction of their responsibilities. This leader knew very little about the responsibilities of some pastors. This list was created by this individual and was lopsided, completely skewed and in error. A quick glance made it look as if the responsibility of the entire church rested on him. Of course his list took up a whole page and under the other pastors – including those in authority over him - were just a few minor responsibilities listed. So on paper, it looked as if this "poor" leader was so over-worked and under appreciated. This leader made sure that the people who served in his department knew about it. In fact, he made sure he carried this list with him in his department binders. None of us even knew about this particular list. We didn't understand why we kept hearing comments from family and friends of how much this person was doing and how many hours he was putting in. It wasn't until after we saw this exaggerated and self-serving list, that everything made sense. This leader got what he wanted, attention.

Another time, during a staff meeting,

we had a time of prayer in the office, and we went around the room individually praying over everyone that day. Weeks later, I find that one of our support pastors (who ended up betraying) was upset that his prayer was not as good as what the others received and let people know about it. That's nauseating! This same leader would regularly ask me to tell them they were doing a good job. Now one time is not too big of a deal, but several times over the course of months is an issue. There is more, but my point is that people with this level of need for attention are never satisfied. They are driven by their own insecurities, jealousies and competitiveness. They feel illegitimate and therefore, use the attention of others to try to fill the void within. When other co-leaders begin to connect with people under the betrayer's leadership or when other co-leaders are promoted in any way, all hell breaks loose! Absalom-style betrayers have difficulty celebrating the promotions and accolades of others on the team because the attention is not on them. They will nitpick, undermine and criticize others while exaggerating their own accolades and self-importance.

7. Rip The Cover Off

What finally revealed Absalom's heart was when he said, *"If only I were appointed judge in the land! Then everyone who has a complaint or case could come to me and I would see that they receive justice."*

Did you catch that? He said *"If I were in charge..."* No matter how hard you try and fight it, your mouth will eventually speak what is already in your heart. Notice that Absalom didn't say "If I were appointed king," but he said "judge." I do believe he was smart enough to not say "king," that could've turned out badly for him. Others would've seen that statement as treason and could've led to an early exposure of his betrayal. Absalom-style betrayers are smart enough to move slowly and under the radar...at least in the beginning. Absalom wanted position and power and he knew what it would take to get it. How sad is it that he was willing to go to the extreme and tear down his father's kingdom.

So many Absalom style betrayers are willing to tear down something in order to gain something for themselves.

Absalom's comment above is subtle, but it was purposed to undermine his leader, gain influence with others and make them question the leader who was in place.

I was helping a pastor work through a painful betrayal from which he and his team were in a bit of clean-up mode. What they discovered was that one of the former pastors made a comment to one of the key volunteer leaders saying, "I'm just not happy with decisions that leadership is making right now." He didn't go into detail, but just enough was said to cause this key volunteer to question leadership. Remember: Absalom-style betrayers are great with their words, they say just enough to inflate others' view of them and cause people to question leadership. Some of the questions that may arise in others may be "I wonder what's really going on?" or "can I really trust them?" This was the case with this volunteer leader. These were exactly the thoughts she was having. Thank God this pastor had the opportunity to clear the misunderstandings up. Unfortunately, this isn't always the case. I give a big shout out to this volunteer for bringing this concern to his pastor's attention. You see, this former leader's comment and tone left it wide open for interpretation and opened the door for vain imaginations to swirl. Absalom used this same tactic with the people, saying just enough to get them to come to him. After all, he was affiliated with the king, king's sons and the leadership.

8. The Betrayer Influence

Whenever anyone approached him to bow down before him, Absalom would reach out his hand, take hold of him and kiss him. Absalom behaved in this way toward all the Israelites who came to the king asking for justice, and so he stole the hearts of the people of Israel.

- 2 Samuel 15:5-6

Absalom-style betrayers will already have some level of influence, but they are never content. They want more! They need more! Why? Because their motives are lust driven, and lust is never satisfied. Absalom would meet face-to-face with the people. He would have the one-on-one meetings (seemingly caring and pastoral) because he wanted to win the hearts of the people. Absalom-style betrayers are more deceptive because they can have an appearance of being "for the people" but they are really about themselves.

What's ironic is that the influence they have was actually given to them by God and leadership. They have been given the opportunity to lead others because the gift was recognized and the door to lead was opened for them. But to the betrayer, it is no longer enough.

To the leader: You can do everything correctly and go through all the proper steps to hire, train and nurture the right person, but you can't do anything about the heart of a person as it becomes entangled like Absalom.

So far, we've read about Absalom stealing the hearts of the people, but as we read further, it's evident that these people weren't enough for him. He needed to go higher up the chain. I'm sure he loved seeing his number of followers grow, but if he could have gotten another top tier leader to side with him - then he would have really had the backing to move forward. It would probably even justify his actions to the other followers and assure his success. An Absalom-style betrayal is only as powerful as the numbers that will follow.

Several years ago, two of our leadership team pastors, along with two other key staff people, left and started a church right down the road. They also took several other great families from our church and caused the biggest split from our local church that I know about to this day. It wasn't enough for these two pastors to just leave; they influenced two other key staff members to go with them, causing even more of an exodus. They probably thought "The greater number of players, the greater the impact." Well, as I said earlier, what is from God will last and what is not, will not...and it didn't. Absalom-style betrayers need a followership, and they will use any means necessary to make it happen. The fallout from such acts is staggering with so many people hurt and no longer involved in the church or connected.

9. Absalom's Followers

Let me make a point about the followers: Sometimes, in the beginning, many of them are innocent and ignorant.

And with Absalom went two hundred

men invited from Jerusalem, and they went along innocently and did not know anything.
- 2 Samuel 15:11(NIV)

Sadly, many great people are unnecessarily ripped from their place in a church or team. I have seen people follow betrayers and wind up completely confused, lost and angry when the betrayer's life or his church goes badly. As a result many of these followers are still lost, wandering around and not connected to a local church today. I've met plenty! Instead of reconnecting to the body of Christ, they have fallen into the deception that they can just be the church all by themselves. That is the lie that the devil would have us believe. I get their point, but it is wrong.

Absalom-style betrayers have a similar kind of people they draw to themselves. Here are some commonalities of people today who will follow an Absalom-style betrayer.

1. A track record - They could have a history of past issues with other churches/leadership.

2. Wounded - They have big trust issues and can easily be persuaded.

3. Vulnerable - They can be extremely needy people and overly interested in conspiracy theories.

4. Gifted - They often serve at high levels in one

or more areas of the church.

5. Popular - They are fairly well known throughout the church. The Absalom style betrayer needs backing and the higher and more influential they are, the better off they are.

Absalom goes for the jugular!

As you read further, you will see the next step that Absalom took in his betrayal against King David-his father.

While Absalom was offering sacrifices, he also sent for Ahithophel the Gilonite, David's counselor, to come from Giloh, his hometown. And so the conspiracy gained strength, and Absalom's following kept on increasing.
- 2 Samuel 15:12 (NIV)

Let's look at the progression of Absalom's betrayal. In the beginning, he had provided himself fifty men and at this point - through lies and deceit - had grown to two hundred followers. As we see, Absalom wasn't satisfied with just having the two hundred followers. He knew he needed more of an influence to do what was in his heart to do. He knew something was missing. He wanted someone of greater influence that would solidify his efforts. In the passage above, Absalom's lust for position and power led him to send for Ahithophel to come meet with him. It is here that these two join together in the conspiracy against David. Both were family to David and he loved and trusted them greatly.

So why Ahithophel? Who was he?

He was Bathsheba's (David's wife) grandfather. Do you get that? He was Absalom's great grandfather on his mother's side. More importantly, he was David's counselor, trusted advisor and his personal friend for years. Ahithophel was someone he could confide in regularly. When David looked for wisdom, he talked with Ahithophel. And this is who Absalom sent for. Being a leader for as long as I have been, I know a person like this is rare; and when God brings someone into my life like this, it is gold and they are cherished!

Look what the bible says about Ahithophel, the grandfather of Bathsheba, whom David stole from Uriah the Hittite.

Now in those days the advice Ahithophel gave was like that of one who inquires of God. That was how both David and Absalom regarded all of Ahithophel's advice.
- 2 Samuel 16:23 (NIV)

So, Ahithophel was David's relative through marriage. Remember: betrayal happens from people that are the closest to us. David and Ahithophel were so close and basically ran the nation together. David could lean heavily on him for counsel, sound advice and direction. We don't read it, but one can imagine David having moments of pouring his heart out to Ahithophel, revealing his fears, doubts, insecurities and being more vulnerable with him than anyone in the land. This was the guy he was able to pour out his deep concerns and frustrations to. David loved him deeply. His trust level for this man was big and I would dare say the most out of anyone in the kingdom. I have a few people I love and trust like this in my life. These kinds of people are rare.

Not all of them betray, but when people this close and this trusted do, it packs a punch and knocks the wind out your sail. It leaves quite the sting. Absalom hit David where it counted, but in the end what counted to God was what stood victorious - The truth! And the same goes for you when you are betrayed. Stay in the truth and watch God move on your behalf. It may not be instantaneously, but trust in him and stay in truth.

It may take a while, but truth always wins.

4. Delilah-Style Betrayers

Our second story of betrayal covers the Delilah-style betrayer. It's about a woman who betrays her husband for possessions. Although this story's focus may be more about a marriage or relational betrayal, it does help us learn so much more about betrayers we may encounter in life as well.

Delilah was beautiful and Samson was strong. In fact, he was the strongest man on the planet at that time. But the beauty and strength outwardly did not mean beauty and strength within. No one else at this time knew where Samson's strength came from, but Samson. I'm pretty sure he would've been the second strongest man if I had been alive at that time. (insert laughter)

The Story

Some time later, he (Samson) *fell in love with a woman in the Valley of Sorek whose name was Delilah. The rulers of the Philistines went to her and said, "See if you can lure him into showing you the secret of his great strength and how we can overpower him so we may tie him up and subdue him. Each one of us will give you eleven hundred shekels of silver."*

- Judges 16:4-5 (NIV)

There are many things that, if asked, I

would simply not be tempted to do. Tempting me to steal or kill someone just simply won't happen. It's not my weakness. However there are some things, that when tempted are a little more of a battle to overcome. It's only by God's grace and strength in the midst of my weaknesses that I have overcome. We all have areas we are strong in and areas we are weak in, but it's those areas of weakness that the devil will periodically battle us in. He doesn't need a big opening to get in, just a crack in the door will do. All the devil needs is for a temptation to stick at the right time. Being tempted is not the problem. We all have been tempted, including Jesus, but he was without sin. Problems happen when temptation connects with a desire deep within. This is why I believe that most betrayers are not evil or they do not start out to betray, but rather a temptation was dangled before them that connected with an ungodly desire and it opened the door.

Read what James tells us:

"But each person is tempted when they are dragged away by their own evil desire and enticed. Then, after desire has conceived, it gives birth to sin; and sin, when it is full-grown, gives birth to death."
- James 1:14-15 (NIV)

I believe this is what happens with people who betray.

I wonder how someone could betray a spouse, a pastor or a friend. How could they hurt someone they say they love? Aside from unresolved issues within, the truth is a temptation was dangled out in front of them. This temptation, over the course of time, connected with an evil desire and gave birth to sin.

Delilah was no exception. She was tempted and allowed herself to be enticed by riches. The end result was that she ended up betraying her husband. Delilah was enticed by the rulers of the Philistines, who at that time, were the enemy. Let me just say that ANYTHING the enemy has to offer, no matter how big or great, will never bring life to you. It may appear wonderful on the front side, but offers no life on the backside. Delilah became blinded by her desires, which drove her to an act of betrayal. The enemy attacked in her weakness, and that is how the devil works. He attacks in our weakness.

Do you know your weaknesses?

Do you know what enticements you have? Do people close to you know them so you can be covered? Make sure you know them so that when the devil tempts you, you can overcome it.

We don't know exactly how many rulers showed up to Delilah that day, but apparently it was enough. Eleven hundred shekels of silver times the number of the Philistine rulers was a lot of money. While Absalom's betrayal was motivated by a desire for position and power, we see that Delilah's betrayal was motivated by a desire for possessions - silver. An argument could also be made that she wanted some position with the rulers. Either way, Delilah's lust for the silver opened the door for her to expose her husband's weakness.

I can only imagine what kind of relationship these two had. Probably pretty heated sexually, but pretty cold emotionally. Samson was a womanizer and had a serious weakness for women, but Delilah was a bit different than the other women he was with. Delilah was the only woman that the Bible tells us he actually 'fell in love' with.

His first wife he really liked and the second woman was a prostitute whom he slept with. Well, not sure there was much sleeping going on. I don't believe he was in love with the first two women. However, the Bible makes it clear that he was in love with Delilah. She was the one he actually opened his heart up to and loved deeply. One thing of importance is that the Bible never makes mention of Delilah loving him. We see that when Delilah betrayed him, it devastated him to the core.

> Remember betrayal can come from people we love or from people who say they love us.

I'm amazed at how much of this kind of betrayal is glorified on tv, tabloids, and reality shows. We see so many family members betraying each other for money, an affair or some kind of possession. For the most part, we can disconnect from it emotionally because we see it so much on tv. We become numb and desensitized to it. However, when we experience betrayal first hand, it is an entirely different story. When a spouse is caught in an affair, or the kids betray their parents for an inheritance, it is reality but it's not a show. The pain can be excruciating and the journey to healing can be long.

Delilah's act of betrayal was not a one-time "oops I made a mistake" moment. Like all betrayers, Delilah was a pretender and very deliberate and persistent in her pursuit of the possession. It's amazing to me how many people trade in the life-long permanent blessings from the Lord for temporary possessions. Look at the persistence it took Delilah to reach her goal.

#1

So Delilah said to Samson, "Tell me the secret of your great strength and how you can be tied up and subdued."

Samson answered her, "If anyone ties me with seven fresh bowstrings that have not been dried, I'll become as weak as any other man."

Then the rulers of the Philistines brought her seven fresh bowstrings that had not been dried, and she tied him with them.

With men hidden in the room, she called to him, "Samson, the Philistines are upon you!" But he snapped the bowstrings as easily as a piece of string snaps when it comes close to a flame. So the secret of his strength was not discovered.

#2

Then Delilah said to Samson, "You have made a fool of me; you lied to me. Come now, tell me how you can be tied."

He said, "If anyone ties me securely with new ropes that have never been used, I'll become as weak as any other man."

So Delilah took new ropes and tied him with them. Then, with men hidden in the room, she called to him, "Samson, the Philistines are upon you!" But he snapped the ropes off his arms as if they were threads.

#3

Delilah then said to Samson, "All this time you have been making a fool of me and lying to me. Tell me how you can be tied."

He replied, "If you weave the seven braids of my head into the fabric on the loom and tight-

en it with the pin, I'll become as weak as any other man." So while he was sleeping, Delilah took the seven braids of his head, wove them into the fabric and tightened it with the pin.
Again she called to him, "Samson, the Philistines are upon you!" He awoke from his sleep and pulled up the pin and the loom, with the fabric.

#4

Then she said to him, "How can you say, 'I love you,' when you won't confide in me? This is the third time you have made a fool of me and haven't told me the secret of your great strength." With such nagging she prodded him day after day until he was sick to death of it.

So he told her everything. "No razor has ever been used on my head," he said, "because I have been a Nazirite dedicated to God from my mother's womb. If my head were shaved, my strength would leave me, and I would become as weak as any other man."

When Delilah saw that he had told her everything, she sent word to the rulers of the Philistines, "Come back once more; he has told me everything." So the rulers of the Philistines returned with the silver in their hands. After putting him to sleep on her lap, she called for someone to shave off the seven braids of his hair, and so began to subdue him. And his strength left him.

- Judges 16:6-19 (NIV)

Manipulators and Information

Delilah-style betrayers are very persistent and skilled manipulators. Much like Absalom, Delilah-style betrayers will use their words and certain tones to get what they want. Notice how many times she asked him for the inside information concerning his strength. She needed to know and used nagging, manipulation and guilt to get it.

Be cautious of people who strive to have the inside information and seem to always "need" to have it. They will use any kind of information to sell out leaders, friends, family and/or co-workers to get what they want or to simply be on top with information. They love to be in the flow of information and they love gossip. These pretenders view information as power. In leadership, Delilah-style betrayers can appear to be hungry to grow and they may even start out that way, but it's really an appearance issue. The information they receive is a short-lived satisfaction on the road to gaining something more.

After several attempts, Delilah was able to weaken and break down the strongest man in the land. He would then be stripped of his gift and calling of God, all for a little silver. That is some pretty good nagging.

>
> The devil doesn't play fair and his goal is to take leaders, ministries, marriages and families down.

I have a friend who lost his whole church, ministry and influence because of this very issue. His wife used information and gained followers to kick him out of his position. Many were hurt, confused and spiritually wounded. To this day, he is not engaged in ministry and the pain is so real. This true story actually has the combination of Absalom and Delilah in it, which is lethal duo.

Back to Samson

Something could even be mentioned here about the naivety of Samson. You would think after two or three times of Delilah's actions, he would have been awakened to her deception. Why wasn't he aware that something was wrong? Was he so blinded by his lust or was he just afraid of losing Delilah? Did he truly see what she was doing and was actually just that passive? Maybe the answers to these questions are all a "yes," but what we need to take note of is the importance of protecting what God has given us. Jesus said, if we are not careful, we will give our pearls over to pigs. Yes, he was referring to people.

"Do not give dogs what is sacred; do

not throw your pearls to pigs. If you do, they may trample them under their feet, and turn and tear you to pieces."
— Matthew 7:6 (NIV)

We as leaders, must be careful to guard what God has given and not hand over information, power, or authority to people who really just want to use it for their own gain. They can be well meaning people, but well meaning people don't get the pearls of my life. They don't get information they don't need. That is reserved only for those who have earned it. Delilah-style betrayers are great at misleading you into believing they are with you and for you, but deep within the recesses of their heart, they are holding onto the rug you are standing on ready to pull at any moment. They can be the kind of leaders who want information, not for the betterment of the ministry or department, but because of their lust-driven needs. Information to them is the vehicle to get them to higher places in the organization. It's like a drug that really never satisfies. Like Jesus said, some people are like dogs and some are like pigs. Protect what he's given you.

I remember some meetings when one of our pastors would persistently tell us how important it was for them to have ALL the information. They would get offended and upset when they found out they didn't know something. This staff member could never tell us why they needed it and could not give a clear answer.

The information they wanted had nothing to do with their department or their sphere of authority and responsibility. The red flag goes up when someone strives with this much intensity for information. Realistically, there was no reason for them to have it. As leaders, we believe in strong communication and want our leaders to have what they need to succeed, but the striving for ALL the information was over the top.

After seeing a pattern develop, we realized there was a deeper issue here, and when we confronted this person they acted out. It was like a volcano of destruction exploded. We began to see deep-rooted jealousy, manipulation and insecurity that led to unhealthy competitiveness with other leaders and it caused division. To us it was sudden, but it really was there all along, hidden deep within the recesses of their heart. So we began removing this person from meetings that didn't pertain to their area and still would only give the information that was needed for success. I learned that day when you cut off a Delilah-style betrayer from the flow of information or meetings they think they need, you must get ready for a battle. The battle is much like we read in Delilah's fourth attempt with Samson.

Delilah-style betrayers who lust for the information will pursue it. It's important to know that no amount of information they receive will ever satisfy. I'm convinced that their wants will never be satisfied because it is lust driven. Lust is only temporarily satisfied and never quenched. When you look at the 'possession' through the eyes of a Delilah-style betrayer, the 'possession' doesn't have to be money. It could be a number of things, such as a position, recognition, or a greater following.

Betrayers are Users:

Delilah's goal was to weaken Samson by the constant nagging and manipulation and she succeeded. Four times she came to Samson nagging and working her emotional string pulling. We experienced similar nagging and manipulation with this particular staff member in saying, "If you trusted me, you would give me the information." Or "for me to be the best leader or pastor I can be, I need to be in on the meetings." A betrayer knows what they want and they are going to get it. Delilah's target may have been the silver, but the information was the vehicle she needed to get it.

When people betray, they will use anything and anyone to get what they want!

Samson remained strong for the first three times Delilah nagged, but then he just had enough. He finally caved in. Look at what the Bible says about it.

With such nagging she prodded him

day after day until he was sick to death of it.
- Judges 16:16 (NIV)

Finally, through the constant nagging, he was weakened. He gave in and told her what it was. She got paid, but lost everything in the end. Delilah-style betrayers may get paid, but lose so much in the end. Both Samson and Delilah died as a result of her betrayal. It's sad to me how many relationships, ministries, businesses, churches and marriages have been destroyed from within because of Delilah- style betrayers.

5. Judas-Style Betrayers

Finally, we have Judas, an interesting kind of betrayer. This guy could very well represent multiple people in our lives. Depending on the angle you are looking from, the Judas-style betrayer could be a close friend who was trusted at a deep level, someone that you have spent years mentoring or poured your heart into, a co-worker and/or teammate, and even an up and coming promising leader or pastor in the church.

Toward the end of Jesus' life, he was talking to his twelve 'hand-picked' disciples about his betrayer. This was a very private and personal setting. He begins sharing about his body being broken and his blood being poured out. So, obviously they all are intrigued.

After he had said this, Jesus was troubled in spirit and testified, "Very truly I tell you, one of you is going to betray me." His disciples stared at one another, at a loss to know which of them he meant. One of them, the disciple whom Jesus loved, was reclining next to him. Simon Peter motioned to this disciple and said, "Ask him which one he means. " Leaning back against Jesus, he (one of the disciples) asked him, "Lord, who is it?" Jesus answered, "It is the one to whom I will give this piece of bread when I have dipped it in

the dish." Then, dipping the piece of bread, he gave it to Judas, the son of Simon Iscariot. As soon as Judas took the bread, Satan entered into him. So Jesus told him, "What you are about to do, do quickly." But no one at the meal understood why Jesus said this to him. Since Judas had charge of the money, some thought Jesus was telling him to buy what was needed for the festival, or to give something to the poor. As soon as Judas had taken the bread, he went out. And it was night.
- John 13:21:30 (NIV)

Could you imagine what it must have been like to be sitting with Jesus and the others or to listen to Jesus say that someone at this table will betray me? I can imagine the awkward silence in the air, as well as the thoughts of unbelief by the disciples sitting there. I can imagine the shock and anger that someone could actually betray Jesus. Who would do such a thing? Who's the bonehead?!

I'm sure the questions and thoughts were stirring in the disciple's minds. The wonder and fear that maybe it was the one sitting at their side. Maybe even trying to figure out if they themselves had done anything earlier that week that could possibly resemble betrayal. Why would someone at this level want to betray? And furthermore, how does he know this?

Betrayal comes from the people who you

least expect it from. Some of you would never have dreamed that they would pull something off like this. In my experience, Judas-style betrayers are genuinely good people. They are people with hearts to serve, love others, and really want to fulfill God's purposes and plans, but once again they are enticed away by desire from within. There's the problem.

What makes this story of betrayal unique from the others is that not only did death accompany the betrayal, but LIFE followed as well. Yes, you heard me right. Death and LIFE appeared on the other side of this betrayal. God used Judas' betrayal to launch Jesus into his destiny. This gives us hope when we are betrayed.

If we allow God to come into our story of betrayal, he will help us experience the life he has for us.

What destiny could be ahead of you as you continue moving forward in the midst of your betrayal?

Will you allow God to be a part of your story?

I believe as we follow Jesus' example and keep our eyes on the Father, life will eventually win in the end. I speak from experience on this one.

The Innocent:

In our first two examples of betrayal, the argument could be made that Samson and David opened the door for their betrayal. I'm not justifying Absalom and Delilah's actions. However, when Judas betrayed Jesus, there is no argument that Jesus opened any door. Jesus didn't deserve his betrayal and neither do people that are betrayed. One of the toughest issues in betrayal is when you are betrayed by someone you love and you did nothing wrong.

Judas was in the inner circle and was personally chosen by Jesus. He knew Jesus up close and personal like only few did. He was one of the fortunate to sit with, be taught by and hear the heart of Jesus regularly. He saw the real and raw side of Jesus. He saw great miracles. He saw and experienced many things that aren't even recorded in the Bible.

So how could this have happened? How could someone so close to Jesus do such a thing? Was Judas so close that he lost sight as to who Jesus was? Did he really ever believe it in the first place? Did he allow the sin of familiarity to creep in? Was he ever really in from the beginning? Did deception just slowly creep in through the years? Was the thought of the money so enticing that he just gave in to it? Or was it just plainly the will of God so that Jesus could finish the work of why he came?

There are so many questions, as there were for me when certain betrayals happened. I believe there are just some betrayals that will happen to us that we will not have answers as to why until later on down the road, if ever. I do believe however, that as you move forward and keep looking to Jesus, he will help you find purpose in it. Trust me, you will see it.

Satan and a Judas

The questions need to be asked. Did Judas' betrayal against Jesus begin at the dinner table that night? Did it begin when Satan entered into him? Did Judas' evil thoughts just get so powerful that he just couldn't overcome them any longer? Did he have an inward battle brewing beneath the surface the whole time and just never said anything? There are many questions surrounding this story of Judas and I surely don't have the answers to all of them. However, I can at the very least bring clarity on one issue.

No betrayal ever just happens and Satan is always working to destroy anything that God is building with his people. After all, Satan is the deceiver and he does three things very well; steal, kill and destroy. If he can deceive one-third of the angels in heaven, he can deceive any of us if we are not careful and alert.

> It doesn't matter how close you sit to Jesus at the table. You can physically sit next to him, but be completely disconnected in your heart.

Jesus answered, "It is the one to whom I will give this piece of bread when I have dipped it in the dish." Then, dipping the piece of bread, he gave it to Judas, the son of Simon Iscariot. As soon as Judas took the bread, Satan entered into him.

- John 13:26-27 (NIV)

Satan may have entered into Judas at that moment, but I am certain there were many inward battles that went on prior to this moment. Some of the battles could have been with doubt, the legitimacy of Jesus, possibly greed or even fairness issues. Satan doesn't have to be in you to tempt you. Temptations will always come knocking, scripture shows us even Jesus was tempted. However in order for sin to be born, the devil needs the right temptation to connect with the right evil desire within to lure us away (see James 1). When we give in to the temptation and allow ourselves to be enticed, sin is born. The only way Judas could've been "dragged away" is because the devil enticed enough and finally connected with an evil desire. If Judas didn't have the evil desire, there would've been no betrayal toward Jesus.

Premeditation

Then one of the Twelve—the one called Judas Iscariot—went to the chief priests and asked, "What are you willing to give me if I deliver him over to you?" So they counted out for him thirty pieces of silver. From then on Judas watched for an opportunity to hand him over.

- Matthew 26:14-16 (NIV)

Notice Judas was the one who approached the chief priests. He's the one who called the meeting and then took the money, and he is the one who looked for the perfect moment to hand Jesus over to the religious leaders. The betrayal actually happened long before Jesus was arrested. The same is true when we are betrayed. Judas' betrayal toward Jesus began in his heart, germinated awhile and then it became public. This is similar to Absalom and Delilah. Because Judas received money for the betrayal... the question remains, was greed the evil desire within? If it was, he surely didn't get a lot from the religious leaders. And to think that Judas went through all this effort and betrayal for only thirty pieces of silver, and a little temporary notoriety. That much silver was the lowest amount paid for a slave in that day. Isn't it amazing how the deception of betrayal will make us think stupidly? Maybe this is how little he thought of Jesus. Then when Judas' guilt kicked in, he tried to return the silver to the religious leaders. So maybe greed was the evil desire after all. Maybe it was this and more. This does help us to become more aware of Satan's workings.

Even while sitting at the table with Jesus, the devil was able to enter and deceive Judas. None of us are above this. All three of the betrayers were dragged away (from truth) by their own evil desires and enticed. Then sin was born. In Judas' case, and in the other two stories, the sin was betrayal.

What's ironic is that Judas, the guy who handled the money in Jesus' ministry was the one who ends up betraying for money. Remember, it's when the temptation gets a hold of a desire. As I said earlier, no betrayal ever just happens. There is always a premeditation of the act.

Judas, one of the twelve disciples, arrived with a crowd of men armed with swords and clubs. They had been sent by the leading priests and elders of the people. The traitor, Judas, had given them a prearranged signal: "You will know which one to arrest when I greet him with a kiss." So Judas came straight to Jesus. "Greetings, Rabbi!" he exclaimed and gave him the kiss. Jesus said, "My friend, go ahead and do what you have come for." Then the others grabbed Jesus and arrested him.

- Matthew 26:47-50 (NIV)

In those days, it was customary to greet a friend with a kiss. How sad is it that Judas displayed the look of a friend but was carrying the dagger of betrayal in his hand (figuratively speaking). Betrayers are very good at playing both sides. Remember, they are pretenders. Judas, who sat at the intimate table with Jesus, was now leading the crowd that wants Jesus arrested and killed. Who would have thought that was possible?

You may think it's just the bad people who betray, but we are all susceptible to falling into the clutches of it. We all have the ungodly sides of us that we have to work through. You know those areas in us that aren't like Jesus yet and those areas that are in process of becoming healthy? This is why we all must stay alert. Now, I didn't say paranoid, but alert. All the devil needs is the right bait. This is why the Bible tells us to stay alert.

Think on this: every church, every marriage, every business, and every relationship is only one person (or one decision of betrayal) away from division. This is not to scare you or make you feel on edge, but its intent is to keep you sober and alert to the enemy's schemes.

From Pain to Glory

Jesus knew that he was going to be betrayed, but just knowing it didn't take away the pain of what he endured afterwards. The same is true for anyone who is in leadership. We know about betrayal and are told that it may happen, but knowing it doesn't take away the pain that follows. Many times it's the people who are in your corner cheerleading the loudest who hurt you the most.

When I took over as lead pastor, so many close friends would come up and say things like "we're with you" or "anything you need, just let me know" or "I'm so excited and ready to move forward." The funny thing is just as soon as we started moving forward as a church, many of these are the ones that just suddenly left the church and some of them took others along with them. I never understood how one week they would be cheering and the next week they were nowhere to be found. I learned quickly to not rely on the praises of man, but rather the voice of God. I had to learn to not get too high with the praises or too low with the criticisms. It is definitely easier said than done.

Even though you know that betrayal can happen at one time or another, it's still painful. For those who think that Jesus didn't feel much pain because He was the Son of God - think again. The truth is that Jesus had to feel this pain to the fullest.

Jesus had a much bigger purpose than this betrayal, and so do you and I.

Like Jesus, we need to begin seeing ourselves beyond betrayal. If Jesus did it, you can too. God didn't cause the betrayal in Jesus' life, or ours. People do that. God does have a way of showing us purpose in it and helping us through it. He does bring healing and will help you get to the other side so that his bigger plans can be seen. Betrayal can and will derail you off your course if you let it. My encouragement to you is, don't let it!

To the betrayed, you must remember that our God still works all things together for our good and He will do it for you. He will cause all of the pain of betrayal that you have been through to work together to make you stronger and fulfill his purposes - both in you and through you. If you truly allow for the healing process to happen, then you will come out golden on the other side and will actually see God's greater plan unfold. Jesus saved the world! Who could you help by following Jesus' example?

To any leaders in the church or in business, if you have been in that position for some time, chances are you have experienced a painful betrayal by someone. It's like it's built into the system. I have found that leaders sometimes experience betrayal more than once. The more I meet and talk with people, pastors and leaders around the nation, the more I see how prevalent betrayal is today. My question has been, is it any worse than it was in the early days of the Bible? I think the only thing that differentiates the two eras is that our present day glorifies it and the days of scripture dealt with it ruthlessly. Betrayers today are paraded as stars and heroes. In Bible days, death surrounded them and was often the result. If you have been 'stabbed in the back' by someone, you don't have to live any longer with the knife still stuck. You need to (figuratively) reach around and pull it out. The wound will never heal as long as you allow the knife of betrayal to remain.

6. Getting Through Betrayal

Poised Under Pressure

When people betray, our response matters. In football, there is a phrase when a quarterback stays under control and focused while under pressure by the defense. It is called being 'poised in the pocket'. Many times, when a young and immature quarterback is under pressure by the defense, they prematurely scramble due to the pressure. This can make for a bad play and can cause the offense to miss the intended play altogether. When a quarterback can stay poised under pressure, he is able to make a more accurate throw. Yes, there are times for a quarterback to scramble, but mature quarterbacks understand the reward of remaining poised (calm) under pressure.

The same principle is true for leaders and people who are blindsided by betrayal.

When we are betrayed, often there is great pressure, confusion, anger, and all the other emotions that come with it.

It's easy to begin scrambling around out of control trying to put out the fires. It's easy for us to get out of sorts and as a result, cause even more problems. My encouragement for you is to stay poised in the pocket when betrayal happens. It is key, and many times, will determine the level of fallout. David did this. Jesus did this. We can do this too!

The number one partner in crime to betrayal is all the lies and accusations that are thrown your way. The exaggerated stories and lies that have been told by the betrayer will make you want to scramble. In my experience, betrayal will typically include more than one lie and more than one person who now believe the lies and accusations about you. In some extreme betrayals, they will come in from all sides. Some of the lies will even make you chuckle a bit. Just know that this is a part of it, and many times, you can't do much to clear them all up. Stay poised while under the pressure. Don't let the pressures of someone's betrayal cause you to scramble and get out of sorts.

God Will Defend You

Years ago, when we experienced a betrayal by a support pastor and close friend, we were completely blindsided by all the lies that were already started by this individual. There wasn't a whole lot we could do to clear it all up. Our resolve was to trust God, and with the many lies all we could do was let it run its course. That wasn't easy! This can be one of the most frustrating sides of betrayal; not being able to right the wrong that has been done to you.

There have been several occasions when we wanted to stand up to defend ourselves. We wanted to clear up the lies, but many times the Lord would not let us. He had us remain silent. Even now, years later, there are random moments when we hear some of the lies that were spread. However, we have learned that defending ourselves simply causes more problems. There are some accusations and lies that are just not worth the headache. Many times, the devil's plan is to get us drawn into a battle that wasn't ours to fight. He wants us scrambling around, not poised under pressure.

God will fight our battles for us if we let Him.

God may not do it the way we want or in our timing, but remember that every word that rises up in judgment against you and I, He will prove to be wrong! In the end, truth always wins. The problem is that many times we have to wait for the truth to win. So while you're waiting, stay poised and trust that God will fight for you.

"The LORD will fight for you; you need only to be still."
- Exodus 14:14 (NIV)

My question for you is: Are you remaining poised? Will you wait long enough for the Lord to fight for you?

A Person of Few Words

As you go through betrayals, you will find yourself in situations when silence or a few words will be your best defense. Be a person of few words or no words at all. You won't always feel like it, but it is what will bring the most life to you and others. Your flesh will want to say or do all kinds of things because we all have that part in us that doesn't like to be wronged. We want it cleared up - right now! We need to set things straight. We want to look good. When betrayal happens and crazy lies and accusations are said, just let your responses be short and sweet. Stay poised in the pocket. Trust that God will work it out for you.

Jesus never defended himself and you don't have to either.

When your desire and action to defend yourself is greater than your desire and action to trust God to defend, you can step out from the protection and covering of God for your life.

Now, there were times that I did have some of the necessary conversations with the necessary people. The conversations I had were about keeping unity and us moving forward as a church and/or team. Being a person of few words and letting God fight for you doesn't mean you retreat or bury your head in the sand. It means to stay poised in the pocket while under pressure. Do what you can do to keep unity and peace, and let God take care of what you cannot.

He is Our Defense!

When Jesus was betrayed by Judas, he was brought before the people in charge and his response to the accusations was short and sweet. Sometimes he didn't defend himself at all. In my mind, this would've been the perfect place and time for him to preach that best-selling sermon or perform the life-changing miracle, but he didn't. He wasn't moved to win the people over in that moment. He had already been doing that for three years. He knew that God was his defense. Look at how Jesus responds when Judas and the crowd came to arrest him.

Jesus said, "My friend, go ahead and do what you have come for."
- Matthew 26:50 (NIV)

Not many words and not combative. He's probably thinking "You have already betrayed me in your heart, so now go ahead and make it public." We can learn a lot by how Jesus responds here – short and sweet.

One day, after a powerful Sunday

morning service, I was approached by a very nice lady who had just moved back in town. We'll call her Evelyn (not her real name). She said she attended our church several years ago, but had run into a former pastor who left our church during a split. We'll call her Silvia (not her real name either). These kinds of meetings are recipes for all kinds of bad!

Well, Evelyn begins telling me some things she had heard from Silvia. What made it that much tougher, was that she said this in front of two other people right there in the hallway. The things that she told me were crazy and I wanted so badly to defend myself in that moment, but I felt the sudden hand of God cover my mouth. So I just politely replied back to her. My flesh (the me place) was screaming inside, but my spirit (the God place) was softly quieting me down.

In that moment, I did not name the person that I knew was responsible for these crazy lies. I knew I couldn't tell the story and what they had done to us as a church. By the grace of God I ended up giving a short answer and covered our church in an appropriate manner. So, in a few words, I cautiously and concisely pointed out to her the truth of the matter. She did recognize it and said that what she experienced during service was nothing like what she heard. God is our defense. It was in this season of crazy lies and accusations that I believe God led me to this scripture.

It is to one's honor to avoid strife, but every fool is quick to quarrel.
                    - Proverbs 20:3 (NIV)

I knew in that moment if I had stepped out and defended myself, I would have been a fool.

Don't be Reactionary!

Many people make impulsive decisions in the midst of pain. How many of us have stubbed our toe and then turn and slam our hand on something because of the pain in our toe? I have. And because of me reacting, I was in pain in two areas. The same is true when we quickly "react" to betrayal's pain. I know those who have made statements like "I'm never going to open up like that again" or "I will never trust anyone with my heart again." Some leaders have walked away from their calling and some have just relationally distanced themselves from others only causing more pain in their lives. Too many never bounce back from being betrayed. They're stuck. They are living life as if the knife is still stuck in their back.

God doesn't want us stuck, he wants us moving forward.

Guarding yourselves from the reactionary thoughts and actions is key. Being reactionary can lead to so many more problems. You know, those thoughts of revenge, quitting and retreating from the thing you are called to do. Even the wrongful thoughts of wanting the betrayer(s) to pay for what they did. Maybe you're in leadership and are battling the thoughts "Is this really worth it?" or "do I really want to keep doing this?"

I remember these feelings when I went through a couple of the most difficult betrayals in leadership. I remember the sleepless nights and the feelings of failure and fear that gripped my mind. I was bombarded with the fears of other friends betraying, families leaving the church and me being exposed as a failure. I remember the anguish that I felt for weeks and sometimes longer. Not only did I feel the attack at a personal level, but at a church/ministry level as well. It was relentless. I really wondered if it would ever end. I had thoughts about just shutting it down relationally and becoming one of those pastors who just preaches from the pulpit, but doesn't have any real relationships. This is the type of pastor that appears one way on the stage, but is entirely different away from it. I could become the pastor who will not let anybody in their life and keeps people at arms length relationally. But I knew that wasn't me, nor is it how I want to be.

Don't Shut Down

I have found that the depth of love for someone parallels the depth of the pain when betrayal happens. This is why it is so painful when people we love betray. So what do we do when we are betrayed? What happens next? Do we ever trust again? Do we open up again? Do we ever allow someone in that intimate place of our hearts or invest into people again? Do we shut down and go into a heart protection mode? I guess these are options, and may be a temporary solution, but the results can be very costly and even deadly.

We can actually function in 'shut down' mode, but we will end up living a pretty lonely and sad life. We will never experience the joy and fulfillment God desires for us. Pastors can still preach in shut down mode, but their influence in other peoples' lives will be very low, if at all. Leaders in shut down mode can even do the job and get tasks done, but when in 'shut down' mode, will disconnect relationally with others and the passion that once fueled them will be gone. Things can even go well for us externally (job, finances, ministry, non-profits,) but those places inside will remain empty of abundant life. When we shut down relationally to people, we will shut down relationally to the Lord. This is not what God desires for us. If we are not careful, we as pastors and leaders will become indifferent to the call of God and in turn, allow the three headed monster to sink its teeth into the heart of your church, team or business. I believe this monster is the deadliest of all and I will cover this in detail in the next chapter.

Pursue Health

We are a three part being, and God desires for us to be healthy in all three - spirit, soul and body. I find that most people pursue being healthy in one or two of these areas. It seems few people pursue all three. The ones that do pursue all three are truly the ones who live abundantly full lives.

Look at what John wrote:

Beloved, I pray that you may prosper in all things and be in health, just as your soul prospers.
- 3 John 1:2 (NKJV)

This is my hope and prayer for you - that your soul (your mind, will and emotions) - would prosper and be in health. Don't put your heart on lock down. You may need a season to repair and heal from the wounds of betrayal, but while in this season, keep trusting. You must keep looking to Jesus as your help and keep going forward until you get to the next season of strength. I promise it will come.

Look at what David writes in Psalm 62. He's writing again about the betrayal that he experienced.

Truly my soul finds rest in God; my salvation comes from him. Truly he is my rock and my salvation; he is my fortress, I will never be shaken. How long will you assault me? Would all of you throw me down — this leaning wall, this tottering fence? Surely they intend to topple me from my lofty place; they take delight in lies. With their mouths they bless, but in their hearts they curse. Yes, my soul, find rest in God; my hope comes from him. Truly he is my rock and my salvation; he is my fortress, I will not be shaken. My salvation and my honor depend on God; he is my mighty rock, my refuge. Trust in him at all times, you people; pour out your hearts to him, for God is our refuge.
-Psalm 62:1-8 (NIV)

In verses 3 and 4, David tells us what is going on in the betrayal. The bigness and severity of having his kingdom possibly toppled, the lies spread that he is not able to clear up, and the two-faced betrayers that are in his life. Notice what he surrounds these scriptures with. In verse 1-2 and 5-7, he declares through faith and trust in God, that his victory in this comes from God alone. And God is the rock on which he will stand.

He is declaring that no matter how difficult the issue is, he is going to stand on the rock - Jesus.

He knows that his victory is from God and when you stand on the true rock, victory will always be yours. Your betrayer may seem to be having victory for a season, but ultimately, the victory is yours. In order for you to have this heart in the midst of your betrayal, you need to learn how to do what David did in verse one. He waited quietly before God. This is so vital in your victory. Believe it or not, with all the other voices and noise going on around you, God does have something to say to you in the midst of it. But you must quiet yourself and listen. For me, it was extremely difficult to wait quietly before the Lord but it was so worth it.

When issues like betrayal happened, the natural pull was for me to engage in a battle to prove my innocence and defend myself against the lies. That's not what God wanted. He doesn't want you and I to go with the natural pull, but a supernatural pull. The supernatural pull is learning to wait quietly before him because he knows that out of waiting on him comes a right mindset and heart set for what is ahead. Lastly, in verse eight, David encourages us to trust at all times, pour out your hearts in prayer, and to know that no matter what is formed against us, God is fighting for us and he is our refuge.

7. Three Headed Monster

So now that we know the three most common betrayers (Absalom, Delilah and Judas) and the three main focuses (possession, position and power) for betrayals, it's time to dive a little deeper and expose the three heart issues that drive people to betray.

The Three-Headed Monster

In 2008 I was asked to take the reigns as the senior pastor. A couple of weeks into serving as the new pastor, I was in my car driving when the Lord asked me a question. He asked me if I wanted to know what I was dealing with in leading the church. What he spoke in that moment would change me, and eventually the church, forever. He shared with me about three issues that have been in the church since it opened its doors thirty years ago. They were: Personal (or competing) Agendas, Selfish Ambition, and Control Issues. I call this "the three-headed monster." While this is just my attempt at being clever, it works. The Lord said that these three issues were in the foundation and DNA of our church and they must be removed. He said that these are the issues that had worked their way into the church and had led to continual divisions, church splits, broken relationships and broken dreams. It was these three issues that led to so much destruction in our church.

I remember this was so unique that

I stopped and wrote it down so I would not forget it. I figured this must be pretty big and powerful if he spoke about these three specific things. I had never heard this said before about our church, but I will say that it was accurate. Based on just the church history I knew, it was spot on. So with this insight, I began a long journey to gain a greater understanding, dive deeper into the issues and to do whatever was needed to remove it.

As I looked back since the time my wife and I started attending here, I could clearly see that the division the church experienced throughout the years did, in fact, stem from these three issues, and when I took a deeper look into this church's history prior to us attending I found much of the same. Now God did many great things in our church throughout the years, but it was in this season that he was serious about cleaning some things up.

The Journey

I had so many questions that I needed to find answers to. I wanted to know how the church started? Who started it? What were the issues in the beginning? What was the original vision of the church? What were the patterns that had continued throughout the years that brought such division and heartache?

I talked with as many of the people as I could who were there at the beginning stages of the church. Many random meetings and divine appointments happened during this season as well. God himself was dictating the schedule. Hindsight would later prove that he was. Out of the blue, it seemed, some of the founding people would show up at our services, or I would run into someone and through simple conversations they would open up and share things. They had no clue that they were being divinely sent with more pieces of the puzzle. Other times, people would write me a letter or come into the offices to talk. Some of these were people who were not even attending the church any longer. I knew these moments were not just coincidences; they were God allowing me to gain insight on what we were dealing with. This allowed for more questions to be answered. One man who helped start the church randomly showed up at the office one day to talk. He had not attended for years, but felt the Lord sent him to share some things. How crazy is that? No one even knew that I was on this quest and yet God would bring people through the doors. I was also able to gain some insight from a few people in our church who were there in the early years. I was amazed at what I learned. I was in awe of the severity and the grasp that the three-headed monster had.

The Bigger Picture

My search into the history of our little "c" church led me to more of a global big "C" Church search. I began looking deeper into the fallouts, divisions and splits that have happened in the churches I attended growing up. I also began to look into other churches across the nation that had run into their own problems. Much of the information I gathered is directly related to this three-headed monster. Although the Lord spoke that these three issues were in our local church's foundation, I began to see that this three-headed monster was running rampant throughout many local churches...too many! The results were all the same: betrayals, division, people fighting for positions, church splits, undermining of leadership, and many other evils.

It is these same three issues (personal agendas, selfish ambitions and control issues) that are also destroying families, marriages, relationships and businesses.

After coaching sports for over twenty years, getting this kind of insight on the three-headed monster was like gold. It was like getting the game film of the other team prior to playing them. This insight helped me see who and what we were up against. As a coach, I like to know who the other team's star players are and what plays they like to run. I like to have a game plan before going into battle. The truth is that no amount of pregame film study takes the place of actually getting out there and playing the game. It's extremely helpful, but it doesn't compare, becase it is easier to practice for an opponent than to play against them. The same was true when trying to move forward and root out this three-headed monster in our church. We may have had the insight on what the issues were, but we still had to deal with it. For me, it wasn't enough to just know what the three-headed monster was, I wanted to overcome it and get it out of our church. I wanted to know what was at the heart of these three issues? What were the warning signs to look for in myself - or others? Could we overcome them and if so, how? How do we get them out of the church and out of our lives? And is it even possible? The question that kept lingering in my heart was, could we see a day where we could have 'no more broken churches'?

Shed a Little Light

In the beginning stages of my search, I began exposing what I knew about these issues. I figured we had to start somewhere. So I got our church leadership together and the long discussions began. So we did what we always did - we prayed, we talked, we worked on our own personal growth, we challenged each other, we talked again, we prayed some more, and we continued to grow! Today you can ask any one of our staff members what the three-headed monster is and they will be able to tell you what it is. I teach and discuss it several times a year so as to never forget. I don't do this to magnify the issues, but to continue growing and refining. Talking about a topic like cancer doesn't glorify it, but it gives us a better understanding of how it works and what this disease thrives on. Therefore we know how to deprive it. This is the same for the three-headed monster, if we don't get an understanding, our churches and families will continue dealing with the same issues for years and possibly decades. We must get an understanding, no matter how uncomfortable it gets.

God said in Hosea 4:6 that his people are destroyed for lack (or rejection) of knowledge. My goal here is to shed some light on this three-headed monster so that we can first, remove it from our own lives and in turn, remove it from our churches, businesses, marriages, homes and relationships.

> If God's commanded blessing flows from unity, then that is what we must all fight for and work towards.

What I find is that many people in the church love talking about unity, but will not do what is needed to build it, protect it and to fight for it. Their personal agendas, selfish ambitions and control issues are just too important.

Can We Really Overcome It?

I don't believe that God would have spoken that day if he didn't intend for us to overcome it. I don't believe God spoke this so we will continually be defeated by it. Last time

I checked, he has called his people to overcome and says that as followers of Jesus we are greater than any influence contrary to his Word.

You, dear children, are from God and have overcome them, because the one who is in you is greater than the one who is in the world.
- 1 John 4:4 (NIV)

Who is it that overcomes the world? Only the one who believes that Jesus is the Son of God.
- 1 John 5:5 (NIV)

Some of the things we encounter in this life are a bit more difficult to overcome than others, but I still believe that ALL things ARE possible to them that believe. I just happen to believe we can overcome these issues that have been there for decades. God doesn't need the most gifted and the most eloquent, he just needs the willing and the obedient to get a task done. So now that we know what the three-headed monster is, where do we go from here? How do you and I overcome this three-headed monster?

The first thing is to get a proper understanding of how the individual heads of the monster operate. What do we watch out for? In the next sections, I'll expose the three-headed monster in detail. My hope is that we, with God's power, can destroy this thing and see more churches flourish rather than be broken apart.

8. Personal Agendas

Personal (Competing) Agendas

The first head of the three-headed monster is 'personal agendas'. The problem is not when we have an agenda, but it is when our personal agenda goes against God's agenda or the leader's agenda. When a person forces or puts their personal agenda above God's, it begins in rebellion. That is where problems occur. The next step is for two opposing agendas to compete with one another. I'm not talking about when we have differing ideas, but agendas. The nature of forcing our personal agendas is rebellion.

The plan for personal agendas is to undermine and destroy the plan that God or God's delegated leader is putting in place. Any agenda that is forced above God's is rebellion and is motivated by selfishness, pride or envy. It will oppose God's agenda or God's leader. It is when someone's personal plan begins to undermine the leader they are under, the team they are serving with, and ultimately God. Unless the person repents and there is some kind of miracle from God, it will result in betrayal, division and fallout.

Personal agendas can also be called

competing agendas because that is exactly what they do - compete. The ultimate and most obvious is what we read in the book of John.

The thief comes only to steal and kill and destroy; I have come that they may have life, and have it to the full.
- John 10:10 (NIV)

First and foremost, we see the most severe agendas battling; which is Satan verses Jesus. The devils' plans will always oppose God's plans. God builds up, the devil tears down. Jesus brings life, the devil brings death. These agendas have been competing since the beginning. When Lucifer (Satan) was in heaven, he was kicked out because he tried to push an agenda that competed with God's. Since that day, his agenda has been diametrically opposed to God's. Thank God that Jesus is still the name above every other name and his agenda always wins over the devil. Other competing agendas we face are things such as law verses grace - religion verses relationship with God - followership verses leadership. God has an agenda for strong marriages and families and the devil has an agenda to tear them apart, leaving them in ruins. There are so many more examples, but I know you get the idea.

There are, however some competing agendas that can be healthy for us; such as sports, education, and even what we learn from the animal kingdom. There are two sides with the same goal (to win), even though they may carry differing agendas as to how to get the goal accomplished. I do believe competing is built into life's system and it can be healthy for us. What causes the unhealthiness is when we let our personal agendas begin to compete in the church and work against the leadership and against God's plan for the local house. The manifestation of personal agendas will always lead to delays in the vision, the advancement of the kingdom of God and can be very damaging to the success of any church.

Several years before I arrived at our current church, a split had occurred between the senior pastor and his son-in-law. The story is that the two had different Bible studies going on the same night in different parts of the church. Now having different classes or studies going is quite common in church, but the problem was that the son-in-law was slowly creating a strong following and his teaching was in opposition to the senior pastor. Over time, this ended up in a church split and approximately 50 people left the church and started their own. Which was a lot of people for that size of church, after twenty plus years of remaining the same size, this church is no longer in existence. In fact it closed during the time of me writing this book. The son-in-law was driven by his own personal agenda, which led to division, broken relationships and betrayal. Again, when someone is moved more by their own personal agenda over the leader they are submitted to, it is rebellion. Two competing agendas cannot exist in the same place for very long. One will stay and the other will leave.

Rebellion and submission cannot co-exist in the same heart, because one is the heart of Satan and the other is the heart of Jesus.

Personal Agendas and Rebellion:

When you think of personal agendas, you need to think 'rebellion'. Look at what the Bible says about rebellion.

For rebellion is like the sin of divination or witchcraft, and arrogance like the evil of idolatry.
- 1 Samuel 15:23

This was written when King Saul chose to do his own agenda and rebelled against God. Because of his rebellion, the kingdom he was overseeing was taken away from him. God dealt harshly with a lot of things throughout the Bible, but the one thing he dealt most quickly with was rebellion - Lucifer, Judas, Miriam, Aaron, Korah and his people, Saul, and more. He doesn't play around with rebellion against his authority. This is not because he is on some ego trip and is afraid of being shown up, but because he knows the damage it can bring to his plans and the hurt it brings to his people.

A person functioning in their rebellious personal agendas will become blinded and will no longer be able to see God's agenda, unless there is a change of heart (repentance). If there is no change, their heart will become more and more hardened by their own personal agenda. No amount of conversations and meetings you have with them will turn it around. Hey, if the Holy Spirit wasn't able to change things privately, chances are they won't change publicly. I have found that once this personal agenda has gone public, it seems all that is left is for it to run its course. These people will believe that what they see is truth, but actually they are entrenched in a self-justified lie, which has resulted in rebellion. Barring a miracle, this is headed for betrayal, division and more broken relationships.

Personal Agendas Between Leaders and Followers:

This seems to be where most of the problems occur in the bible. Again, God doesn't deal too kindly with people who operate out of rebellion.

I do want to recognize that there are some extenuating circumstances that happen when a pastor or leader does leave a church and it is not considered rebellion. I realize not all the issues are so black and white. I know that there are some bad leaders in position of leading churches, but I also know that we don't always get to pick the leader we serve under, the timing of our launch and the place where we serve. If you are a support pastor submitted to a lead pastor or a lay leader serving a pastor and you feel it's time to leave, do it gracefully and with some maturity. You don't need to create a following to justify your actions. Just get the heck out and go do what is on your heart to do. If the senior pastor cannot or will not give you his blessing, move on and don't speak negatively. Do nothing but bless the place and leader you served.

The body of Christ has experienced way too much hurt over the years because of this rebellious personal agenda issue, and we need mature leaders and pastors who are willing to put an end to it. The world is supposed to know that we are followers of Christ by our love, but sadly they know us more by our division and the fact that we can't get along. You can have your agenda, that's not the issue, but when it is birthed out of rebellion and begins to compete and oppose the leader that God has placed over you and who you are called to submit to, that's when it becomes a problem.

Having a difference of opinion is not the same as having a competing agenda. You can have a difference of opinion and not walk in rebellion to leadership and cause division. You can think differently and not rebel. You can talk out your opinion and then submit to the ultimate decision of the leader. Trouble comes when one begins to form alliances and create a following so that their agenda overpowers the leader's vision. In order for us to not allow for the divisiveness of our personal agendas to get in the way of God's vision, there must be submitted hearts at the table. Personal (competing) agendas can only thrive when there is rebellion in the soil of our hearts.

Rebellion always begins as a simple seed, growing over time and if not exposed and rooted out, it will eventually manifest itself weaving its tendrils like a choking vine.

Opportunity Denied:

In addition to me pastoring, I also get the privilege of coaching high school baseball. One day I was teaching a player something about his hitting techniques and the varsity coach pulled me aside and asked me to teach it a different way. He wanted me to teach it his way. I will admit that my pride was hit a bit, but God always has something to teach us. God helped me see that if I continued teaching my way, then that was allowing the first head of the three-headed monster to operate within me. I knew that in order for the program to get better and to become successful, I needed to train the kids the way the varsity coach would like, no matter how much of my pride or ego was hurt, it was his program. My job as JV coach was to help these kids get ready for the next level. I could have nodded in agreement to the varsity coach and continued to do my own thing, or I could have submitted and did what he wanted to help build the program. Well, it was an easy decision. I knew enough and had seen enough to know that the only way for this baseball program to be successful is for me to submit and do what was better for the program. So the opportunity for my personal agenda to flourish was denied. If I were to allow rebellion to exist in this simple area, what other areas would I allow it to exist?

Honor His Authority

If we are going to honor God with our lives, we must honor those he has placed in authority over us. When rebellion takes place against delegated authority, it's the same as rebellion against God himself. Remember, God dealt with a lot of things throughout the Bible, but the one thing he dealt with quickly was rebellious personal agendas. It's the hard-hearted, arrogant, immature person or leader who thinks they can rebel against God's delegated leadership and still expect his blessing on what they do. What I find is that many people are not mature enough to sit down with leadership, talk it out, and wait to be released with a blessing. They force an issue, create a church split and never experience God's full blessings on their work. In my research, pastors who start another church out of a split will either stay close to the same in numbers that left with them or they will eventually shut down. God's blessing simply cannot and will not be on rebellious church split start-ups.

Overcoming our rebellious nature is something that I believe will always be in process. Rebellion is a heart issue and so is a forced personal agenda.

If a person is rebellious in the simple things, they will be rebellious in the bigger things.

Many things are connected to the heart of rebellion – pride, ego, selfishness, jealousy, just to name a few. It's the person that smiles and nods their head in agreement at meetings, but is not in agreement at all behind the leaders back. It's the worship leader that thinks the senior pastor is not spiritual enough and leads the worship team away from the pastors' vision. It's the support pastor who takes the people they are leading in a different direction then the church is going. These leaders may do their job, but they have another underlying agenda that slowly pulls other people away from each other and unity; which in turn, keeps them from God's commanded blessing. We see this with Absalom-style betrayers when they believe "I know what's best" or "if only I was in charge". When there are people on staff, or in key leadership roles, with personal agendas, unity becomes impossible. Therefore, God cannot command his blessings over the church. Read Psalm 133. It seems that no matter how many good ideas the team may have and begin, they don't seem to have much success. I find they continually hit the invisible brick wall.

King Saul

There are many stories throughout the Bible that show us competing agendas and what it leads to. When King Saul rebelled and competed with God's agenda, the kingdom was removed from him. I have seen many pastors and leaders rebel against God's delegated leaders and end up being in the same boat as Saul. They may still do some ministry here and there, but not at the same level. It is truly the picture of a gift being in operation without the anointing on it. Many of the pastors or leaders who did this are not even in ministry any longer. I know that God still loves the people, but the truth is that God cannot and will not bless something born out of rebellion. It's an issue that must be exposed and dealt with at a heart level. Rebellion is something conceived or birthed without God's blessing or seed in it.

Seeds of Betrayal

Miriam and Aaron began to talk against Moses (behind his back) because of his Cushite (Ethiopian) wife, for he had married a Cushite. "Has the Lord spoken only through Moses?"

they asked. "Hasn't he also spoken through us?" And the Lord heard this.
- Numbers 12:1-2 (NIV)

In verse one, Miriam and Aaron begin using Moses' wife as the main reason for their gossip, frustration and private meetings. Verse two shows us the real issue. Their problem was not that their brother married a Cushite woman, their problem was that they lost sight of God's agenda and they began operating out of their own. When the real issue eventually manifested itself, it came out in crazy accusations, complaints and frustrations; which resulted in gossip and rebellion. This same thing happens with people who have operated from a personal agenda. It isn't clear in the Bible how many conversations Miriam had behind Moses' back, but apparently it was enough that it was time for God to step in. With Moses present, God called for a meeting with Miriam and Aaron at the temple. Miriam was rewarded with leprosy and set outside the group for seven days for her rebellion. It was a public discipline that other people in the camp knew about and could see...but would they correct it?

Four chapters later in Numbers 16, we see what happens when simple seeds of rebellion grow and mature.

Korah son of Izhar, the son of Kohath,

the son of Levi, and certain Reubenites—Dathan and Abiram, sons of Eliab, and On son of Peleth—became insolent and rose up against Moses. With them were 250 Israelite men, well-known community leaders who had been appointed members of the council. They came as a group to oppose Moses and Aaron and said to them, "You have gone too far! The whole community is holy, every one of them, and the Lord is with them. Why then do you set yourselves above the Lord's assembly?"

- Number 16:1-3 (NIV)

As we read, they had not learned from the punishment that Miriam received for her rebellious personal agenda issue. They saw her get leprosy. They watched as she was separated from the camp for seven days. Apparently, this wasn't enough to get their attention. Rebellion makes you blind and makes people think that the lie is actually truth. Korah and the others were so blinded by rebellion they couldn't clearly see the accusations and complaints they brought against Moses were dead wrong and could not have been further from the truth. Read below what the Bible says about Moses.

Now Moses was a very humble man, more humble than anyone else on the face of the earth.

- Numbers 12:3 (NIV)

So how could the most humble man on the planet be lording his position over the people? The truth is that he wasn't lording but he was leading.

Strong leadership doesn't mean a proud heart, just like someone who serves doesn't necessarily mean humility.

Strong leadership is what's needed, and when it's shown, people who operate out of these three issues will not like it. Remember that betrayers always spread outlandish lies and accusations. Well, this is that!

When rebellion is in the mix, people don't think straight or see clearly. Korah and his 250 men lost sight of God's agenda and began getting their agenda in the way. They had forgotten that not so long ago they were slaves in Egypt and under the enemy's authority.

This rebellion of Korah in chapter sixteen was actually the manifestation of the seed that Miriam sowed just a few chapters earlier. It all stemmed from comments from the previous conversations that Miriam and Aaron were having with Korah and the others behind Moses' back in chapter twelve. Even though God dealt with Miriam for those seven days, the seeds of rebellion already were planted and continued to grow from there. It's scary and sobering how Korah and the two hundred prominent men could all come together to complain and accuse Moses. Maybe they felt that if they all came at once, then their agenda would overpower Moses'- which actually was God's agenda. Now read what happens as Korah and the other two hundred and fifty rebelling leaders verbally come against Moses.

But 14,700 people died from the plague, in addition to those who had died because of Korah.
— Number 16:49 (NIV)

One person's (Miriam) words of rebellion and sowing seeds in others led to almost 15,000 dead people. This is how serious God deals with us forcing our rebellious personal agendas. We may not see death like this today when people act out in rebellion, but we do see death come to many of these people in the form of broken marriages, unrealized dreams and visions, broken trust, wounded faith, and even the calling of God on their lives thwarted. It's amazing how many people follow blind rebellious leaders. Many of them today are not connected in church or even serving God any longer. They say things like "I still believe" and "we just have church by ourselves". Let me just say, that is not God's plan for the church.

The word church is a plural word but with a singular understanding. It is many parts unified to make up one body of people called out by God to reach the world. The writer of

Hebrews tells us to not neglect meeting together. I don't believe you can be the church all by yourself. You need us and we need you to make up the body of Christ, no matter how much we may frustrate each other from time to time.

In this time of Korah, the place where God's people were camping was called Hazeroth; which means the place of craving. The people began craving for something other than what God wanted. This can happen to all of us if our cravings for position, power or possessions become larger than our craving for a personal connection and submission to the heart of God.

Like Korah, people today who operate out of personal agendas hurl accusations to undermine the leader's authority.

People with personal agendas won't work alone and they will most likely have a following. They will refuse to believe they are in any kind of deception and more times than not, there will be no repentance when confronted by leadership or even when disciplined by God.

So what to do?

The only thing to do is to separate yourself from these people. Look what Moses told the people.

> Then the Lord said to Moses, "Say to the assembly, 'Move away from the tents of Korah, Dathan and Abiram.'" Moses got up and went to Dathan and Abiram, and the elders of Israel followed him. He warned the assembly, "Move back from the tents of these wicked men! Do not touch anything belonging to them, or you will be swept away because of all their sins." So they moved away from the tents of Korah, Dathan and Abiram.
> - Numbers 16:23-27 (NIV)

Not only did God tell the people to get away from their tents, but he said to not touch anything that belonged to them. Pretty serious stuff. As I said earlier, God deals harshly with rebellion. If he says move away from these people, then DO IT! Even Paul tells us the same things.

> I urge you, brothers and sisters, to watch out for those who cause divisions and put obstacles in your way that are contrary to the teaching you have learned. Keep away from them. For such people are not serving our Lord Christ, but their own appetites. By smooth talk and flattery they deceive the minds of naive people.
> - Romans 16:17-18 (NIV)

> If they still refuse to listen, tell it to the church; and if they refuse to listen even to the

church, treat them as you would a pagan or a tax collector.
- Matthew 18:17 (NIV)

There is a reason that God tells us in the Bible to separate ourselves from these people. He knows how cancerous these issues of rebellion and personal agenda are. If you are a pastor, it is important to know that people who betray you and cause division through personal agendas will pull people from your influence. Those who are pulled will not be able to fully submit to your leadership and your vision while at the same time remaining connected to someone who has launched out in their personal agenda. Some may still attend and stay serving for awhile, but if their connection remains with the ones who have caused division, they will eventually separate from you. That is why a clean break is needed. Lastly, when God deals with them, you don't want to be around it at all.

Characteristics:

Below are some of the characteristics of a person who operates out of personal agendas.

• These people will typically be in higher-level places of leading. Lucifer was God's worship leader. Miriam and Aaron were family and close to Moses. Korah was a part of the team of pastors(priests), Judas sat at the communion table with Jesus.

- The contentment and joy they once had is no longer present in what they do. The lust for more has taken over. They see more. They want more. They must have more.

- They refuse to submit to the leader. This is the person who no longer can submit in his heart to the senior pastor or leader and their vision. They may go to meetings and look like they are together outwardly, but eventually the rebellion within will be exposed. Rebellion has slowly eroded their heart and their ability to submit and trust.

- Constant reminding - This is the person who continually needs reminders of the vision and game plan. The constant reminding is not for clarity's sake, but because they have the inability in their heart to connect to the bigger vision.

- They lost the passion. The passion to advance the kingdom they once had has drastically declined. Their calling has now become about just getting a paycheck and maintaining for a position or status.

- They will argue about simple things. They will make small issues into big problems. It's very similar to how Miriam and Aaron created an argument about Moses' wife, which really wasn't the issue.
- They no longer have honor and reverance for the leader they are under. They have no

problem speaking against the leader and do so often (Num 12:8).

• They don't like true team ministry. They are not good in a team environment. They become easily threatened by other leaders who bring good ideas to the table. They can't and won't celebrate other's successes.

Important to Know:

Throughout history and even now, when God's people stayed unified and followed God's agenda, they experienced supernatural breakthroughs and victories.

When they didn't, they lost every time and great destruction happened. When God's leaders followed God's agenda, he and the people succeeded. The idea is to stay submitted to the leader you are under and submitted to God. Hopefully you can see that leadership is no walk in the park. We will never become a perfect leader, but we can be 'on-purpose' in pursuing perfection.

9. Selfish Ambitions

The second head of the three-headed monster is selfish ambition. Whenever the words 'selfish ambition' appear in the Bible, we find they are listed among words of great sin and evil. In 2 Corinthians 12:20, the Apostle Paul writes with great concern. He was concerned, based on what he was hearing, that when he showed up he would find the following: discord, jealousy, fits of rage, <u>selfish ambition</u>, slander, gossip, arrogance, and disorder among the people. Not a very positive list. We also see when Paul wrote to the Galatian church (Galatians 5:20-21), that selfish ambition was listed among other not-so-positive words such as: hatred, discord, jealousy, fits of rage, dissensions and factions, envy, drunkenness and orgies. He says that those who live like this will not inherit the kingdom of God. James simplifies it for us.

For where you have envy and selfish ambition, there you find disorder and every evil practice.
- James 3:16 (AMP)

It's hard to believe that these words were actually written about a New Testament church. We're talking about a church that Jesus is looking to marry. A church that has been saved by grace. A church that Jesus died for. A church that Jesus wants to present to the Father. If someone showed me this list, and I didn't know these passages of scripture, I would never have connected them to the bride of Christ. Sadly enough, they were in fact, written to the church - both in the early church and to the churches today.

During my journey of learning about the history of our local church, I could see where just about every one of these issues listed above had manifested. In Philippians, when Paul wrote for us to do nothing out of selfish ambition, he meant it – do nothing. And it appeared to me that we were doing many things out of selfish ambition.

Do nothing out of selfish ambition or vain conceit. Rather, in humility value others above yourselves.
- Philippians 2:3 (NIV)

What is it?

The truest definition of "selfish ambition", also known as carnal ambition means "strife" or "rivalry" and comes from the Greek word eritheia. It was used in secular Greek to describe "those who electioneer for office or a position." They are the ones "who strive for popular applause of people by trickery." The Ancient Greek describes eritheia as "mercenary self-seeking" and "acting for one's own gain," regardless of the discord (strife) it causes.

The heart motives of a person who functions out of selfish ambition are pride, self-love, and self-advancement. It is the drive to put themselves ahead of others or to 'one-up' others. They are notorious for spinning the truth in order to look good and get what they want.

> Selfish ambition will always be a barricade and a destroyer of unity within a church, family or team.

The two (selfish ambition and unity) will never co-exist very long. One will win and one will lose. That is the nature of selfish ambition.

Relational Issues

Have you ever known someone who has a pattern or a history of broken relationships? I'm not talking one-time issue, but a pattern. These are the ones who for some reason have a trail of relationships gone awry. The fault is always the other person(s), but yet there is still a trail. They can go to different churches, different cities, a different marriage and still the result is the same - broken relationships. People who operate out of selfish ambition will have a trail like this. Their relational issues may be separated by a few years, but when you look at their track record, you will find this is a pattern. Strife seems to follow them. Could it be that this person is motivated by selfish ambition?

Church Leadership Issues

People who serve and lead within the church and who are driven by selfish ambition are sometimes difficult to spot. They are not necessarily the ones who stand on the tables yelling "look at me" or "I am full of selfish ambition." No, these are the ones who on the outside look like the serving hero. They are the ones who can greatly serve, but be motivated by selfish ambitions. Below are just a few characteristics of a person who operates in this way.

• They will have a driving need to serve or lead in many areas of the church, but their need is to be noticed.

• They are the so-called all stars because they can seem to do it all. Other people will make comments about how much they are doing in the church and people driven by selfish ambition love hearing it. They can use this as fuel to create problems in the future. Their mode of operation is to take on more and more responsibility, but later will blame the leaders for their own striving and grappling.

• They are bouncers (not in a bar). They typically won't serve in just one area for any great length of time. Their pattern will be to leave a department when the newness wears off or they will bounce to wherever the excitement is.

• They are attention seekers. These people

need to be seen. They will get involved in the areas that are getting the most attention. If their area is not getting the attention, they will attack the area that is, or go after the leader directly. Sometimes they will go serve in that area as well, or exaggerate stories in their own area so as to get the attention. (Have I said yet that they like attention?) They like to be noticed and strive to get the highest levels of position possible within the church. They have a difficult time doing what they do before the audience of one – Jesus.

• They are glory hounds. They do not like sharing the glory with others. They will actually take the credit for the things that they never did. These people will have a difficult time truly celebrating the successes of others unless they are being celebrated too. Many times their selfish ambition issues arise when someone else is promoted and they feel they should have been given that position.

• They love the praises. They cannot go too long without the praises and pats on the back. These people pout, play the push-pull game, exaggerate stories within their department or life and/or their workload so as to increase the praises of people. It is kind of nauseating.

• They have an unhealthy competitive nature. These people do not like to be outdone, and won't be. If they feel threatened by someone else on the team, they will slowly try and take them out. They will undermine other leaders, cross lines of authority and outright lie. They want people to know about their authority and skills. A person like this will do everything in their power to remove or limit the threats.

As a leader, I love people who are go-getters and get things done, but what makes it difficult is that more times than not, the selfish ambition is not usually revealed until further down the road. What makes it even more difficult to spot is that not all the people who serve in multiple areas and lead in high levels are motivated by selfish ambition. However, it's only a matter of time before people who are motivated by selfish ambition are revealed. Over time, their words and actions will reveal what is really going on inside. They may give a big amen for unity, but their actions toward it will not match up. The people they are leading disconnect from other co-leaders or pastors. The Bible says that all sorts of evil and vile work will exist when selfish ambition is at work. Eventually, undermining leadership, entitlement, lying, misleading others, exaggerations, and strife will lead to division, broken relationships and betrayal. Their action of serving does not necessarily mean they are serving for and with the heart of Jesus, but only time will tell. Remember, 'who people really are will eventually show up.' Lay leaders or support pastors can lead or serve for a long time before this issue manifests. Sometimes it was there from the beginning and sometimes it is developed over time.

Leaders who operate out of selfish ambition will over time leave a trail of strife with others.

Some signs to guard yourself from:
* Do you have a difficult time serving in a team setting?

* Do you need to be noticed?

* Do you allow yourself to get to high with the praise of people and too low with their criticisms?

* Do you feel you are in competition with co-leaders around you?

10. Control Issues

So far we have covered personal agendas and selfish ambition, but what about the control issues? Control issues are the feelings, thoughts and actions that will continually battle for our surrender to God's plans and his leadership in our lives. This issue is typically the most talked about in the church and probably the easiest to spot. Usually, we can see extreme control in operation because the people who lead with control will operate mostly out of fear and intimidation. They will overpower others through words, their knowledge of spiritual things and their length of time serving or attending a church. They will display a pattern of "one- upping" the other co-leaders and people on their team.

They are horrible at teamwork. When someone makes a statement, their statement will be a little better or just a bit more spiritual. They will not be outdone. They will also form alliances to display power. They need a following and agreement and many will agree because of the fear and intimidation. Their whole drive is to be in charge, to be right and to be the one who knows the information. Watch out when God begins to shift their position and/or authority, all hell will break loose.

It's important to note here that not

everybody who is in oversight has control issues and not all strong leaders are controllers. There are tremendous people that God has put in leadership who aren't driven by control. The ones who stay in a right place though, are the ones who stay submitted to God and his leadership. They are humble in word and in action. They are ok when change happens. They may not like change any more than the others, but their hearts are different and they are able to make adjustments the right way. They will pursue and build unity throughout the church. They will ask the questions for clarity's sake, not to prove someone wrong. They are the ones who can continue to serve not just for a position, but to please God's heart. They do what they do before the audience of one - Jesus. The problem occurs when leaders who are driven by power and control begin to lose their grip on what they think they control.

The Abuse of Power

One main characteristic of a leader with control issues is that they will abuse their power. People with control issues have been referred to as Jezebel in the Bible, and rightfully so. Jezebel was evil and a control freak. She was married to Ahab the king, who was weak hearted and weak minded. He was a spineless leader and he was a thumb sucker. Jezebel was not someone to mess with. She would intimidate, threaten, kill and destroy anyone who stood in her way. Basically, she wore the pants and Ahab wore the skirt in the relationship.

One day Jezebel found her husband Ahab pouting in his room because he didn't get the vineyard he wanted. So she stepped up to get it for him by having Naboth (the owner of the vineyard) wrongfully accused and killed. She set up this elaborate scheme and lie against Naboth and abused her power to get it.

So she wrote letters in Ahab's name, placed his seal on them, and sent them to the elders and nobles who lived in Naboth's city with him. In those letters she wrote: "Proclaim a day of fasting and seat Naboth in a prominent place among the people. But seat two scoundrels opposite him and have them bring charges that he has cursed both God and the king. Then take him out and stone him to death."
- 1 Kings 21:8-10 (NIV)

Here we see that she used an authority that she never had. Ahab acquiesced his authority, which left the door open for someone else to pick up. When a leader doesn't step up, confront, lead and use their God-given or delegated authority, it can lead to all sorts of problems such as: undermining, overstepping responsibilities, intimidation and more. The only way Jezebel is able to operate is because Ahab is in his room sucking his thumb pouting and not on his throne leading. He was not in his rightful place as a leader and so Jezebel was able to move in and abuse both their powers. Even though Jezebel had Naboth killed, look at what the Bible says about Ahab.

(There was never anyone like Ahab, who sold himself to do evil in the eyes of the Lord, urged on by Jezebel his wife. He behaved in the vilest manner by going after idols, like the Amorites the Lord drove out before Israel.)
— 1 Kings 21:25-26 (NIV)

Where there is weak leadership in a church, business or home, the soil is right for the three-headed monster to operate.

Here's a sobering thought: God will hold the leader responsible for what he is called to do and didn't do.

The Loss of Power

Saul also abused his power when God began removing his authority as the king. He started thinking and acting crazy. Look at what he told his guys to do.

Saul told his son Jonathan and all the attendants to kill David.
-1 Samuel 19:1 (NIV)

Enraged with jealousy and anger over David (the newly anointed king), he told his attendants and his own son (who happened to be David's best friend) to kill him.

Change and Control

People with control issues have a need for people and things to be the way they want it. They are inflexible. They don't like change unless they were the ones who made it. God forbid if leadership at a church replaces the pews with chairs or paints the halls a different color, or if they make a change from reading a song out of a hymnal to reading them from the screens. Brace yourself if leadership ends an area of the ministry that is not in line with the vision or is not making an impact any longer.

I heard a story about a couple that had suddenly left a church they had been attending. The pastor was a bit concerned because he hadn't seen them, so he went to visit them at their house. He was blown away as to the reason why they left. The reason? Brace yourself! It was because when they had a potluck dinner, the gravy was not put in right place on the table! I'm sure your wondering if this is some kind of joke, but I assure you it isn't. This is the truth. They left because the gravy was not placed right according to her. I couldn't believe this when I heard it. Now that's a good one. Talk about some control issues.

You find out who has control issues really quick when a change is made that affects them personally.

Years ago, we had someone leave the church because I made a catastrophic change in the service when I took over. I turned down the lights in the auditorium a bit during the worship singing. I know I know...I'm such a rebel. Prior to me taking over, we had changed the name of our church and many people left because they just couldn't handle it. Our pastor, worship, vision and mission were still the same, but because the name on the paperwork and sign was different, they left. Over a decade later, I still see people out in the community who refuse to call our church by the new name. What is that? It's their way of staying in control. We had several families leave the church when we began making some necessary changes in our children's ministry. Our desire was to create an environment that made kids excited to come to church. We wanted them excited about bringing their friends to church. We were creating an environment where kids could meet and learn about a real Jesus on their level. Well when we made some simple changes, you would have thought we brought Ozzy Osborne in to teach the kids.

If changes are made and people with control issues are not in on the decision- making, they will resist it and others will know about it. They will either leave or make it extremely miserable for the pastor.

A pastor was sharing with me about a couple that had suddenly left his church. This couple had once been a part of their volunteer leadership team. On their own accord, they stepped down from that leadership role and began serving in another role. Well, one Sunday they approached him immediately following the end of the message to tell him they were leaving. One of the main issues they shared was that they were no longer a part of the decision making. He had to laugh a bit, because He said they never really were. The problem was that they wanted more control and couldn't have it.

You will always find out who has the control issues when changes are made. I tell our leaders that when they make a change in their area, one of two things will happen – the people will change with you and get on board or they will change areas or even change churches. I don't like it, but that is just how fickle and weak-minded we are sometimes in the church.

Now not all controlling people are in what I call the extremist category. Some people can lead and serve for a long time. They can camouflage their control issues, until a change happens; especially change that directly impacts them. Change is a trigger for a controlling person to manifest. For the most part, these people are fine just as long as you do what they expect or consult them if there is a change. After all, they feel they know exactly what should happen and how it should go, even though they have no responsibility or authority in that area. They can't see how the decisions will affect the church down the road.

Back to Saul

Saul didn't act out in his control issue until God made a change and began removing the kingdom from him. When his control issues manifested, he began despising the one he loved so deeply - David. Out of his rage, Saul began pursuing David to kill him. He would've been happier to see David dead than for him to get his spot. I have seen people who operated out of extreme control issues who would rather have seen the church go under, than to see the church succeed. I was amazed at the vile and evil that would come out of people. People in the extreme control category will even show their agreement or disagreement by what they do with their tithe. If they release it, they hit the like button. If they don't release it, it's the unlike button for the leader.

They Don't Like to be Confronted

As a leader, I know when a spirit of control is at work when I confront someone and I feel the wave of intimidation and fear overwhelm me. This wave of intimidation isn't about whether we like to confront or not or whether we are even good at it. This is about intimidation gripping you and fear holding you back from doing what you know you should do. Many pastors end up quitting or their vision dries up, all because of a few controlling people who may pay the bills at the church.

Although the appearance of a controlling person is strong, stable and in charge, when these people are squeezed we find they are insecure, inundated with self-doubt and fears. They are able to mask these issues by what they do and how they lead. One of their biggest fears is for others to see the real them. Their overbearing leadership, powerful words, and appearance of control can be their mask and they will do everything they can to hide behind it. When challenged, they will puff out their chest even more. Their initial reaction will be anger and defensiveness. Unless there is humility, get ready for a battle.

> When Saul was confronted because of sin, he was defensive and angry and lost the kingdom.

When David was confronted because of sin, he showed humility and repentance and kept the kingdom. What I have found is when leaders with control issues are not confronted, it will slowly suck the life out of that area of ministry and potentially, the pastor and eventually the church. Other leaders will feel intimidated to confront a leader who is controlling.

Controlling People Feel Threatened

People with control issues become threatened when someone who may be just as, or more gifted in their area steps up and others take notice. When they lead an area, they are usually very poor delegators and like to do everything themselves. They will only delegate small insignificant tasks that they really don't want to do anyway. They can be a go-getter and a doer, but they aren't very good at working with others or delegating tasks or projects of significance. They can be motivated by insecurity and fear so they lead or serve in their areas with a very tight grip. This can lead to an 'us four-no more' mentality and end up sucking the life out of that area. I have seen women put a strangle hold on the leadership of the women's ministry and no body was getting in. They were the team. They were it and don't mess with it. When it was confronted, their response was that there just wasn't room at the table. These controlling people will make comments or give the impression "this is MY department" and "This is MY area of service and don't mess with it". Worship team members can be notorious for this.

Years ago, we had a long time member serving in an area that they were obviously not wired to do. Eventually something needed to be said, but who was going to have the conversation? I remember at a staff meeting discussing this issue as a leadership team. We talked more about how we were going to handle the fall out from this persons' response than we did about bettering the overall church. We spent more time on this person's control issues rather than us bettering that area of the ministry. Well, the conversation was had and the person ended up leaving the church. It didn't matter how nice and encouraging we were, this person who was driven by control could not hear it. Everything we would say, they heard through the filter of fear, scarcity and threat. One more time, change is usually the trigger to set a controlling person off. I will say that this area of the ministry is so much better today, but it's sad that a church has to lose someone for this reason.

Trust Relinquishes Control

We can operate out of control issues when we forget where we came from and what God has done for us.

I love that God set up a system of salvation that says the only way we can be saved is to let go of our control over our lives and let God be in control. The only way to truly let go of your control and to allow God to have control is to trust. Trust that he has more than enough provision for you and that he doesn't know lack. Trust that he has your back. Trust that he has your best interests in mind. Trust that he is not holding out on you. Trust that when he closes a door, he will open another one. Trust that when he removes something from your life, he has something much better for you. Trust... Don't control! When you truly trust God, you will trust the leaders he has placed over you. When we refuse to trust our leaders, we typically have a trust issue with God.

Characteristics

* Controlling people will usually have around them weaker people who won't challenge them much and when they do, they are often labeled "disloyal."

* Controlling people will typically not have in their group another strong personality or controlling person. The two will not be able to co-exist, unless one submits or comes under the other person's authority.

* Controlling people like to make comments to demean others so as to keep themselves one step above the others.

* Controlling people are easily threatened and they can tend to walk in a level of paranoia. They will battle with thoughts that someone is after their position. Fear is at the core of it.

* Controlling people are often concerned about their image... Jezebel looked out from her ivory tower and loved barking out orders. She looked good from her window, but don't get too close. They will keep people at arms distance.

* Controlling people will have a very difficult time when their area they could once control is no longer controllable. When a leader is not able to control things any longer, issues arise. For instance, when God begins to increase the church in size or even the area they are leading, a controlling person typically will have issues with this. They can have a tough time with new people or new policies.

* Controlling people feel entitled. After all, they deserve this because they have been here a long time or they know better.

* Controlling people do not create safe environments for others on the team. When a safe environment is created, differing opinions are wanted, even though they may not all be used. When a safe environment is created, healthy disagreements and debates can be had without a major church or team split.

When a safe environment is created, people feel covered when they succeed or even when they fail at a project.

Wrapping It Up

This three-headed monster (personal agendas, selfish ambition and control issue) may seem a bit overwhelming, but it can be defeated. With God's people rising above their own selfishness and learning to walk in unity,

IT IS POSSIBLE! There are many churches that are doing this now. I'm so thankful ours has made the decision to. I believe we will be able to live under God's commanded blessings in our churches, homes and businesses. However, in order to experience his commanded blessings, we must do our part and stop dividing. We must make the decision that we not be the one that betrayal and division comes through. We must have the heart that says 'no more broken churches.' Others may betray and divide, but you don't have to. You can be one that stands to love, protect and pray for Jesus' bride.

11. We Can Beat It

Now that we have covered betrayal, the three betrayers, their three goals and the three-headed monster, let's tackle how we defeat this monster. It may seem a bit overwhelming and appear unattainable, but I assure you it is possible. As I said earlier, I don't believe God would have revealed what this three-headed monster was if he didn't intend for us to have victory over it. We as people of faith must believe that it's possible, no matter how much this monster has weaved itself into our lives.

When the three-headed monster is in operation, the results are devastating. This is why it must be dealt with and not allowed to operate. As leaders, it is devastating when we continue to allow these issues to remain in operation. Let me remind you of the cost of not confronting and allowing this monster to remain; continual undermining, jealousies, divisions, dishonor, lies and betrayal. Some places (like ours) experienced multiple church splits, an exodus of people, and delays in the vision. The three-headed monster will grow like a vine, weaving itself throughout the church looking to land in the most influential areas. Eventually it will squeeze the life out of the organization, no matter how great or small. Defeating the three-headed monster cannot be done only by prayer, but with truth-led and spirit-led decisions. Prayer is essential. Fasting is essential. But wisdom and action are needed as well.

Starve This Monster

In order for us to remove the stronghold of the three-headed monster, we must understand what is at the core of it. We must understand what feeds it?

So the answer to that is... drum role please. It's US! It's you. It's me. It's self. It's our selfishness. It's the me, my, mine, and I. It's about the 'my' calling. My spotlight. My solo. My teaching. My ministry. My gift. My class. My position. My anointing. My opinion. It's when we allow our plans to become bigger than God's plans. It's when we refuse to walk in humility and remain submitted to the leaders He has placed over us. I think you get the point. The life source for the three- headed monster is selfishness.

So, if betrayal and the three-headed monster really need selfish people and selfish hearts to operate, don't be selfish! How about we as God's people make a decision together that we will starve this monster by living unselfishly. Remember what the three-headed monster is: personal agendas, selfish ambitions, and control issues. All three of these issues point to selfishness and it's the selfishness that needs to die within us all if we are truly going to lessen the amount of betrayal and broken churches moving forward. I know this is easier said than done, but no matter how difficult, we must let the Holy Spirit deal with our selfish nature. Refuse to let things be all about you.

It starts with you!

Here is a great truth to remember:

> You and I are loved, called, cherished, usable and valuable to God and people, but you and I are not the greatest thing going.

If you truly want to defeat the three-headed monster, you can. Thank God he cares about this issue even more than we do and he can help! But the question is, "Will we cooperate with the Holy Spirit"? This is not the time to make a list of all the other people that need this information. First, the focus needs to be personal, because defeating it starts with you. As I have taught this to churches, teams and people, some of the comments have been "it seems impossible" or "it's so overwhelming." And truthfully, it can appear that way. With so many people, churches and businesses who operate in the three-headed monster and with the increase of betrayal in our world, how can we defeat it?

My answer is simple: One person at a time. One family at a time. One church at a time. God just needs the 'one' that is willing and then great changes can happen! Are you that one?

It's easy when we read information like this to be thinking of others that need this, but before we will get to help others, the first area of focus needs to be us. The first area of focus becomes you and asking God to help you in these areas of personal agendas, selfish ambitions and control issues. The question to ask "Is there a betrayer inside of you?"

When I began this journey, I knew that I wanted God to remove the selfishness from my life. I didn't want anything in me that would give place to the three-headed monster! I had to allow God and others to speak into my life and reveal my blind spots. It wasn't easy, but it was right. I knew that for me to make any headway in this area at our church, defeating the three-headed monster needed to start with me!

Clean Up

If you're a pastor, or any kind of leader and you recognize the three-headed monster operating in your church or teams, it may be time for a change. Now before you begin confronting and dealing with people, let me encourage you to take some time and make it a matter of prayer and fasting. Then after you have some insight and clarity, begin communicating with the leaders at the top of your organization. Everything flows from the top, so let the change begin with you and then your staff and key leaders.

I am so blessed that I have such a strong wife and a great staff that were willing to allow God to make the necessary changes in us during this season. I knew it had to start with me and then us as leaders and then the rest of the church would follow. I knew I couldn't teach this to the church, without having God work the issues out of me and other staff and leaders. I believe this is the reason that our local church has become a place that is honoring to God and is becoming what he wants it to be. We actually get along and love each other. We are unified on a vision. We do prefer one another. We want to see each other succeed. We aren't perfect at it, but we are moving in that direction. Stating that we get along now may sound funny, but when the three- headed monster was in operation in our church, these things were not seen much.

The Cost

The length of transition and the amount of intensity you'll experience when confronting and exposing the three-headed monster is directly related to how long your church, business or home has allowed for this monster to operate.

For us as a church, it was three decades of personal agendas, selfish ambitions, and control issues we were putting a stop to. We were tired of betrayal after betrayal. We were tired of seeing people being hurt and wounded and knew a change needed to be made.

The three-headed monster was embedded in the foundation of our church and this is why the betrayals, divisions and hurts would keep re-appearing. When the Lord revealed this truth to me about our church, his word was clear. "It has been in the church since the beginning and needs to be removed." If you are a pastor and see the three-headed monster operating in certain people and are going to move forward to confront these issues, know on the front side that not everyone will like it. Some who operate in these issues will fight it and will resist the changes, especially if you as a leader have allowed it to operate for a great length of time without confronting the issues.

People and Change

It's been said, and I agree, that people don't like change, but that doesn't mean all people. I have found that there are many people who do like change, especially when it is for the better. When we began making some necessary changes and cautiously confronting the three-headed monster, we had many who resisted and left the church. At the same time, we also had many great people who stayed with us. The three-headed monster hates change. Change is the biggest reason that causes the three-headed monster to rear its ugly head and manifest.

>
> When we as leaders bring change, people will either change and evolve or they will change by leaving.

You may even have to let some staff go. Who knows? For us, the issues of the three-headed monster were buried deep in the foundation of our church. It's as if God broke up the foundation so a new one could be poured. He wanted a new foundation that wasn't filled with the all the selfish ambitions, personal agendas and control issues of people, and so did we. In order for this to be removed from our church, it wasn't about just sweeping off the old foundation or patching the cracks. It was about replacing the old with the new. And let me tell you, behold... He did a new thing! I wasn't all that joyful during the season of replacing the foundation, but I'm so glad he did it. I love the new heart, focus and character in our church that he has established. I am so grateful the old is gone.

Many times during the foundation re-pour, it felt like the house was being destroyed. Even though God never allowed that to happen, there were some tough, dark days. Today the house (church) is stronger than ever! The cement for the new foundation is not only poured, but it is cured. Some repairs on the house needed to be done, but we are vibrant and alive again - advancing the kingdom and back to it being all "for his glory" and not for ours! We are reaching people who need Jesus and developing strong followers. As I said before, we actually get along and love each other!

We read earlier that when God dealt with Korah and his rebellion, about fifteen thousand people died in the purging. For us it was several hundred people who ended up leaving. Unfortunately, that is often the bi-product when God does a restructuring within a church. When you begin making necessary changes, some people will leave for the right reason and unfortunately, some will not. Some will leave because there is just too much change happening. Some will leave believing peoples' lies, rumors and end up getting caught in deception. Some just get caught in the wake of other peoples' decisions. And for some it is just their time to transition. You must believe, as a leader, that you are doing the right thing by confronting and dealing with this three-headed monster. The next generation of people, youth and children you are called to lead will be so grateful you did.

As a pastor, you will find out very quickly just how deeply the three-headed monster has weaved itself within your church as you decide to move forward. Maybe it's not a foundation issue for you. Maybe it's just an area or two that have been left alone and not confronted. Maybe for months or years, you have tolerated the selfish ambitions, personal agendas and control issues of some because...well, they get the work done or they pay the bills. Maybe their influence is strong and you don't want fallout or anyone to leave the church. I understand all these, but leaving it alone doesn't make it go away. It just gives it longer time to weave its vine throughout more people and more places within the church.

You know the ones you are leaving alone are the same ones who are continually leaving a trail of strife, control and division. The only time they are in line with the vision is when it satisfies them. They can't seem to get along with others for very long. Maybe by now you already see some areas that need to be dealt with. You need to know on the front side the depth of the root that connects the three-headed monster will determine the shaking that happens in your church.

When my wife is transitioning her plants from one place to another, the bigger the root, the bigger the stirring of the soil. For us, we had a lot of soil stirred up. It was like kicking a hornets' nest over and over, and all we did was begin to talk about what the three-headed monster was. I didn't line up people and confront like some wild, out of control leader. I didn't even realize how embedded this issue was, but I found out. Now, I don't believe every person will need to be purged and I don't believe every church will need to go through the extremes we had to. The pastors and leaders who are not going to step up and defeat the three-headed monster will continue to have issues of betrayal, division, strife, and control. It's important to note that the issues may not be constant, but over the course of time, you will notice patterns of these issues operating. There are seasons that this monster appears to be sleeping only waiting to be awakened.

What Is Needed?

Overcoming selfish ambitions, personal agendas and control issues will require three things. These are much easier to preach, and sing about in church, but much harder to actually live out the way Jesus asks us to. They are nearly impossible if you are a selfish person.

The first thing is humility. We must learn how to walk or clothe ourselves in 'humility'. Secondly, we must practice the "one-another" lifestyle. Thirdly, we must choose unity. I'm convinced this will require the work of the Holy Spirit in our lives. We may not be born into this world with these characteristics, but we are born-again with them. So it is possible to live out these three things.

> When you received Jesus as your Lord and Savior, his heart invaded your heart and the Holy Spirit came to empower you to do what you couldn't do prior to following Jesus.

Humility

Humility must become more than just a topical study or pretty word we use. It must become a lifestyle, and this takes a heart transformation. Contrary to what some may believe, humility is not weak. Humility is not soft. It doesn't mean walking around with our shoulders down and a sourpuss face. Humility doesn't mean we have to be broke, beaten down, and limping around in this life. It doesn't mean we let people walk all over us. It doesn't mean we give away our authority or spiritual royalty. It doesn't mean we live under our spiritual and natural position as followers of Christ. True humility is us living a Christ-centered, Spirit-empowered life with the understanding of who we are, whose we are, who Jesus is, and who others around us are.

True humility says: "I am only saved because of the grace and goodness of Jesus". It says "I am not the only gifted person in the group, but one of many." Humility says "It's not about me, but about those around me." Humility says "The only reason I do what I do anyhow, is because God chose me." Humility says "In order for my spiritual gifts to be of any real value, I need different gifts around me." Humility reminds us where we were prior to knowing Jesus, and gives us the patience and love for those who aren't where we are yet. Humility says "I once was so screwed up, lost and broken, but Jesus found me and healed me."

Take a brief moment and fill in the blank line for you. Humility is _____.

Humility is the key. It is the kryptonite to the power of the three-headed monster. It weakens the "personal, selfish and controlling" areas we have. The Apostle Paul tells us to clothe ourselves with humility, not just to memorize and sing about it. Jesus prayed that we, as the body of Christ would become one just like he and the Father are one. For us to clothe ourselves in humility takes time, effort and a work of the Holy Spirit within us. The selfish (carnal, flesh) places of our hearts have to die and the God parts (fruit of the spirit, spiritual, new man) have to continue growing. These two sides will always battle each other, but they won't dwell together. Selfish ambition and humility cannot hang together. Personal agendas and humility cannot live together. Control Issues and humility do not go together. One will lessen and the other will increase. As you continue growing in the things of God, the selfish and fleshly areas will die. If you refuse to grow, then your selfish side will flourish destroying humility. My decision is made to continue growing in God, how about you?

Learning to "One another"

Becoming a "one another" follower of Christ is not at all easy, but is so needed in the church today. It doesn't just happen through prayer, but just like humility, requires effort, understanding and purposeful decision to change.

The heart of humility will look for ways to "one-another" others, but the one who operates in the three-headed monster looks for ways to "one-up" others. Remember, a betrayer is focused on possessions, power and/or position and when the three-headed monster is operating, they will step on whomever to get what they want. They are driven and blinded by the selfishness within. God is looking for the people who will learn, practice and make the decisions to 'one another' in the church. Look at what the Apostle Paul mentions in Philippians Chapter 2.

Therefore if you have any encouragement from being united with Christ, if any comfort from his love, if any common sharing in the Spirit, if any tenderness and compassion, 2 then make my joy complete by being like-minded, having the same love, being one in spirit and of one mind. 3 Do nothing out of selfish ambition or vain conceit. Rather, in humility value others above yourselves, 4 not

looking to your own interests but each of you to the interests of the others.
- Philipians 2:1-4 (NIV)

Man, if we did this alone there would be no way that the three-headed monster could operate. If we looked out for each other's interests, we wouldn't give any place for all the betrayal we see. Unfortunately, this is a great scripture to preach, read and underline...but how many really live this way? I know I want to be one who does and have made the decision to continue moving toward the goal. Aside from the Holy Spirit's power and leading, there is no way this will happen. If your heart is to be more like Jesus, learning and practicing the "one-another" lifestyle is key!

What could happen in our churches, businesses and families if we practiced the "one another" lifestyle?

What if we lived to "one-another" each other rather than to "one-up" each other? What impact could and would we make in our communities and the world? Imagine the joy we would bring to the heart of the Father? How many would connect or re-connect with the church in a deeper way if we got this? My belief is that people who are far from Jesus would come to Jesus in a greater way if we as people of God would live this out. It is possible, but it won't be easy! People, if we are going to stop the betrayals, the divisions and defeat the three-headed monster that is continually destroying our churches, we must learn to operate in true humility and allow the 'one another' lifestyle to manifest through us. Below are nine ways that the Bible shows us how we are to "one-another" each other. What area(s) may you need to step up your "one-another" game?

Serve

You, my brothers and sisters, were called to be free. But do not use your freedom to indulge the flesh; rather, serve one another humbly in love.

- Galatians 5:13 (NIV)

I know some people have a gift to serve. It's how they are wired. They get up in the morning thinking about how they can serve someone. For others, this is not the case. What you must realize is that we ALL are called to serve one another. Not just when we feel like it. We are to serve others because it pleases the heart of God and when you do, you are more like No matter how high you move up in the church or organization, keep a servant's heart. No matter how long you are a follower of Jesus, stay serving others. If Jesus can say "I didn't come to be served, but to serve," then we can too.

Honor

Be devoted to one another in love. Honor one another above yourselves.
- Romans 12:10 (NIV)

To honor, means to value and esteem. When we honor one another, we are valuing others. To dishonor means to treat as ordinary. If you honor and value the body of Christ (church), you will protect it. You won't betray, divide or destroy what you value. People who divide in the church do not honor the church... and therefore do not honor Jesus.

Love

"A new command I give you: Love one another. As I have loved you, so you must love one another. By this everyone will know that you are my disciples, if you love one another."
- John 13:34-35 (NIV)

Love one another appears sixteen times in the New Testament. I imagine it is pretty important to Jesus and therefore should be to us.

Forgive

Bear with each other and forgive one another if any of you has a grievance against someone. Forgive as the Lord forgave you.
- Colossians 3:13 (NIV)

It may take awhile to get over it, but you'll never get over it if you don't start now with forgiving. Remove the heaviness of bitterness by forgiving right now.

> Let's be honest. Some things are much easier to forgive, but all things are forgivable with God's help in your life.

Accept

Accept one another, then, just as Christ accepted you, in order to bring praise to God.
- Romans 15:7 (NIV)

It's easy to accept others who you agree with or who agree with you. It's easy to accept those who are like us for the most part. But can you accept those who are less spiritual than you... or God forbid more spiritual? Will you accept those who are different from you? The healthiest churches and the healthiest people are those who learn God's heart of acceptance.

Agree

I appeal to you, brothers and sisters, in the name of our Lord Jesus Christ, that all of you agree with one another in what you say and that there be no divisions among you, but that you be perfectly united in mind and thought.
- 1 Corinthians 1:10 (NIV)

What could and would happen if we agreed with one another on the things that mattered most?

Harmonize

Live in harmony with one another. Do not be proud, but be willing to associate with people of low position. Do not be conceited.
- Romans 12:16 (NIV)

We can only truly harmonize with each other when we realize that we aren't the best thing going. That we are only a part of the whole.

When I sing and I'm asked to sing harmony, my job is to support the lead, not to force my voice to the front.

True harmony in the body of Christ can happen only when we clothe ourselves in humility and practice this "one-another" lifestyle.

Bearing With

Be completely humble and gentle; be patient, bearing with one another in love.
- Ephesians 4:2 (NIV)

This word bearing with one another means that we forbear one another's issues. Forbearance is a bi-product of the Holy Spirit being evident in our lives. This means as the body of Christ, we are called to cover one another rather than go around exposing one another's issues. I know the exposing part can be more exciting and adrenaline filled, but it is also so much more damaging to others. Not to mention damaging to you! The next time you step out to expose some one else, I pray the Holy Spirit stops you right in your tracks. You'll be glad he did.

Submit

Submit to one another out of reverence for Christ.

- Ephesians 5:21(NIV)

Submitting to one another requires great humility.

When our leaders are younger or less experienced submission requires great humility. Consistently staying submitted to each other is impossible if we refuse to clothe ourselves in humility. And without the help of the Holy Spirit, forget about it! The key is keeping a healthy reverence for Jesus, then we will respect his house, his leaders and his people. The only thing that keeps us from submitting to one another is us. Remember the essence of the three-headed monster is 'us.'

Let me close this section by saying that

reading this and even underlining these passages is not the answer. You can even highlight verses in your bibles with pretty colors, but if they are not part of who you are, they mean jack squat! What brings the changes in your life is when you ask the Holy Spirit to help you in these areas. Then watch the opportunities you will have to humble yourself and "one-another" someone.

Unity

The bi-product of us living in humility and practicing the "one-another" concept is exactly what God is looking for, and that is unity. This must be at the forefront of our minds and we must realize it is key for us to sustain long-lasting victory over this monster.

Every church I know that is doing great things for the kingdom has unity at the top levels of leadership, and therefore is experiencing unity throughout the body. I mean churches of all sizes and styles.

Look at the emphasis that God places on it in the Bible. The Holy Spirit showed up on the day of Pentecost (Acts 2) because a group of people "chose" to stay put and stay in one accord until the promise was fulfilled. In Psalm 133, God commands his blessings where there is unity. Nehemiah and the men rebuilt a place that was in ruins for 141 years in just 52 days. That only happens when people are in unity. The phrase "one accord" (which means unity) appears 11 times in the book of Acts. Ephesians 4:3 states that we are to make EVERY effort to keep the unity of the Spirit. I'll say it again. Jesus prayed that we would be one as He and the Father are one. Unity is throughout the Bible and it is what God desires. It is not God's responsibility. It is ours.

What would happen today if we all could stay put and remain unified? Would we have more moves of God within our churches? Would we see more people follow Jesus? Would we see the church influence in ways they never dreamed of? Unity is key and we must pursue it. I believe unity can change the world. I still believe that God's commanded blessing is where unity is and I am so thankful that I now see it landing once again in our church. Honor God today by choosing unity.

I realize this idea of humility and walking in the 'one another' principle may seem a little far-fetched, but these people do exist today. It's the people who continually allow the Holy Spirit to work within their lives. We will never arrive at perfection while on this earth, but we can allow him to complete his work in us. Ultimate perfection will come when we are standing in front of Jesus face to face. But until then, keep working, keep maturing, and keep moving towards it. I am confident that if you are serious about doing your part in defeating the three-headed monster, the Holy Spirit is ready to help you. Just ask him.

12. Getting Beyond Betrayal

I want to spend a few minutes again on betrayal. Maybe you have been through it yourself. Maybe people have turned their back on you and you have been wounded. Maybe someone close to you has stabbed you in the back. Maybe the betrayal has you somewhat paralyzed inside. Maybe your vision is blurred? Or maybe you have lost the passion in the call or in life. I want to throw you a lifeline so you can get back up.

You don't have to stay stuck because of something someone did to you.

Remember Judas' betrayal against Jesus? Why didn't God stop it? Why didn't God step in to make another way? Judas was one of Jesus' hand selected guys, so does this mean that Jesus was a bad chooser of people? Did he lack discernment? Was he blind to Judas' issues? Maybe if he would've prayed more. Maybe if he did a little less ministering, he might not have missed this with Judas. Maybe if he had deeper worship, this would have never of happened. You see, this is what happens when we are betrayed. We have numerous nagging questions that linger in our minds. But let me just answer these above questions. No, Jesus didn't pick the wrong guy. No, he didn't lack discernment. No, he wasn't blind. No, he didn't need to pray more. The truth is that Jesus was not surprised at all. God is never shocked by any of it and knows it is coming. Even though we may be blindsided by betrayal, God never is.

A great lesson we can overlook if not careful is how God used Jesus being betrayed. What happened as a result of it is remarkable. How the final chapter reads is world changing.

What we see is how God launched Jesus into the next phase of his purpose and the reason for which he came to earth.

Think about this: If Jesus wouldn't have been betrayed:
* We wouldn't know forgiveness.
* We wouldn't have an empty tomb.
* We wouldn't have an empty cross.
* We wouldn't know grace and mercy.
* We wouldn't have the penalty for our sins paid in full at the cross.
* We wouldn't have personal access to our heavenly father.
* We wouldn't be able to call ourselves sons and daughters of God.
* We wouldn't have Jesus currently seated at the right hand of the father praying for us.
* We wouldn't have a defense attorney (Jesus) standing up for us when the enemy accuses us.

I'm sure there are many more things we

could list here, but what we can't overlook is the greater purpose that God revealed as a result of the betrayal. God is a pro at taking horrible issues and making something so awesome out of them! Just to clarify...God did not cause the betrayal, Judas did. What God did is use it to advance his plans and to bless so many others as a result. I know God can and will do the same for you. I speak from experience.

As I look back at the betrayals I've experienced throughout my life, I can see how God has used them to launch me to his greater purposes. It didn't make sense then, but it does now. I now know a much deeper power and freedom of forgiveness. I now know the sweetness of grace and mercy like never before. What's really crazy is how much I learned about God's love for me in a more personal way. I now have a greater perspective on what is the eternal and the temporal. As much as I loved the church before, I have a much deeper love and passion for the church than I ever dreamed of.

With every betrayal that happens in our lives, there is potential for a newly found purpose, new seasons, and new chapters in our lives. You won't get to these places unless you refuse to remain stuck in the pain and choose to get beyond the betrayal. So, I ask you. What could God do in and through your life as you move beyond betrayal? How could your horrible story turn into a powerful message of triumph that someone else can be changed by?

> I believe victory, breakthrough and a new chapter in your life hinges on your decision to move beyond betrayal.

Out of the Ashes

One of my favorite songs over the years has been "Our God" by Chris Tomlin. In the verse it reads "into the darkness you shine, out of the ashes we rise." This is exactly what God did during the darkest seasons of the betrayals. He shined and helped me rise up out of the ashes that betrayal caused. As I pursued health, the result was a better me. If you let Him, He will make you stronger and better through it all - a better friend, dad, mom, pastor, husband, wife and more. If your focus remains on what the betrayer has done, or what the betrayer is getting away with, you will stay living in the ashes of broken down places. Too many wallow around in the ashes of what happened and live in self-pity and revenge, playing the victim rather than the victor. They live with unhealthy anger, resentment and bitterness because they can't seem to get their eyes off the betrayer. Don't let this be you!

Danger

One of the great dangers when you

stay focused on your betrayer is that you may begin to believe the lies and accusations more than believing the truth. When your focus is stuck on the betrayer, more of your attention and energy will be on what they seem to be getting away with rather than how God wants to help you. You can see clearly where your focus and attention is by listening to how you share your story. Are you sharing past betrayal stories from years and decades ago with anger, resentment and hatred as if it happened yesterday? I know some who still share stories from five, six, and even ten years ago as if it happened yesterday, so filled with the hurt and pain. I've heard statements such as; "look what they have done to me" or "they need to pay" or "I'm here because of what they have done." Hey, some of that may be true, but it doesn't mean you have to remain there.

Today, if you are living your life so focused on your betrayer, chances are that you are wallowing in the ashes of a betrayal.

Let today be a turning point for you. Let today be the day you make a change. Wash off the ashes and let God begin a new work in you. Turn your focus and your mind toward Jesus. The Bible says to look up to where your help comes from (Psalm 121) and those who keep their minds stayed on God will be kept in perfect peace (Isaiah 26:3). That's what I want for you, perfect peace. More importantly, that is what God wants. Maybe you have lost a ministry, a position, years, your confidence, reputation, and it just seems too difficult to get back up. Let me tell you that you can! You can rise up from where you are and be rebuilt into something greater than you've ever imagined. You can be restored to a greater place than you were prior to the betrayal. When Judas' betrayal led to Jesus being beaten and crucified, it didn't look like any good could come out of it, but it did! Look at him now. He's alive and doing very well! And the same goes for you. If you keep moving forward, you will rise up out of the ashes and be made into something unbelievable. You will eventually be able to share your story without all the pain, hate, bitterness and revenge, but you have to do your part.

Acknowledge the Pain

Whether you have experienced one or multiple betrayals, you know very well the pain that comes with it. When someone you love and trust betrays you, the pain is real and can be severe. Whether someone that you have poured your life into turns and stabs you in the back or you find out your spouse has been unfaithful to you. It's not easy to get over. The problem is, most people don't know what to do with the pain and many end up stuffing it inside.

Earlier, we covered Absalom and

Ahithophel's betrayal against King David. Well, David was no stranger to expressive writing and in this next passage he writes about the pain and agony he experienced when he was betrayed. Read what he writes:

"If an enemy were insulting me, I could endure it; if a foe were rising against me, I could hide. But it is you, a man like myself, my companion, my close friend, with whom I once enjoyed sweet fellowship at the house of God, as we walked about among the worshipers."
- Psalm 55:12-14 (NIV)

David never mentions any names here, but his writing leads many scholars to believe that he was writing about Ahithophel. David loved him greatly and spent years serving alongside him. And then Ahithophel suddenly joins Absalom in the betrayal. David experienced betrayal first hand. He knew the wounding and the sting that comes with being betrayed. He knew what it was like to have to work through forgiving a very close friend and family member who went behind his back, spreading lies, causing others to turn against him, and stealing from him. In the next passage, we read more of the pain and sorrow that David experienced from the betrayal. Look at some of the wording used in Psalm 55 as he writes from his heart.

My thoughts trouble me and I am distraught because of what my enemy is saying, *because of the threats of the wicked; for they bring down suffering on me and assail me in their anger. My heart is in anguish within me; the terrors of death have fallen on me. Fear and trembling have beset me; horror has overwhelmed me.*

- Psalm 55:2-5 (NIV)

I want to make sure you capture the moment here in Psalm 55. David is doing something here that is sadly a lost art. He is being vulnerable and transparent. When something as painful as betrayal happens to us, we have a choice on how to respond. We can either shut down, lock up areas of our hearts (which is a breeding ground for bitterness and hatred) or we can choose to begin a journey of vulnerability, forgiveness and health. Personally, I have responded both ways throughout my life and I can say that choosing to forgive is the way to go. David was very good at expressing his heart in writing throughout the Psalms. David's vulnerability and openness has now helped millions of people today trust God in the midst of tough situations. Oddly enough, in my roughest season of betrayal, I read this chapter and was deeply encouraged. Maybe it was just knowing that I wasn't alone. Maybe it was being in good company. Maybe it was seeing what David went through and knowing if he made it out on the other side all right, then I could also. Thank God that David was willing to be real enough to do this.

Look at some of the words David uses above to describe what is he is going through: trouble, distraught, threats, suffering, anguish, terrors, fear, trembling, horror and overwhelmed. David uses ten heart-wrenching words to best describe what he was going through. When I look at this I can't help but see a man so hurt, so broken, so lonely, so shocked and devastated by what has happened. I see him desperately trying to communicate what he was feeling. I see him giving his best attempt to accurately get out on paper what's going on inside. I see him alone in one of his chambers trying to write as tears roll down his cheeks. The anger, shock, sadness and confusion, all wrapped up in these few verses. I wonder how many times he tried writing this. How many pieces of paper were balled up and thrown over by the trashcan? For those of us who have experienced betrayals, we can relate. I can remember the overwhelming number of thoughts and feelings that I wrestled with. I know all to well, the extreme emotions that followed being betrayed.

Are you open to acknowledging the pain that betrayal has left? Or will you do what many do and continue stuffing it inside to the point you become emotionally constipated? Let's take a moment and use King David's example. If you're in midst of a betrayal, write down ten words that would describe the pain you are experiencing.

1. _____
2. _____
3. _____
4. _____
5. _____
6. _____
7. _____
8. _____
9. _____
10. _____

Moving forward

> Getting beyond betrayal is a step-by-step journey and requires courage, strength and faith to get there.

If it were easy, everyone would be on the other side of betrayal, but this is not the case. This journey is not an exact 1 + 1 = 2 formula. All of our stories of betrayal are unique and therefore all our healing journeys will be unique. But I have found these four steps or practices help across the board and can accelerate your journey into a new day. They may sound simple in word but they are not simple in action. These have helped me tremendously in my journey and I pray they help you as well.

1. You are not alone

Betrayal can be isolating, but it doesn't mean you have to remain isolated.

Jesus, Paul, David and many other pastors, leaders, and people have gone through betrayal and came out golden on the other side. But sadly, many are still stuck in the pain of betrayal. Make a decision right now that you will get up and get moving forward. Find someone who is further along than you and talk it out. See a counselor. Talk with someone who doesn't know the story and can look at the situation objectively. I am so glad I did. It was the best thing I could have done. The more you talk through the betrayal with the right person(s), the quicker you will get moving. Your story is unique, but you are not the only one who has experienced betrayal. Don't camp out in the "poor me" place. It will take time to work through the emotions and the pain, but over time, you will come out stronger and healthier.

2. Focus on the bigger picture

Betrayal can be devastating, but you don't have to continue living devastated. The betrayal you've experienced doesn't have to destroy you. It doesn't have to keep you from your destiny. With God in your corner and the right people around you, you will make it through it. He will help you become bigger, better and stronger. It may not seem like it right now, depending on where you are in the journey, but he will. Jesus experienced great pain, but he was able to keep his eyes on the bigger picture of his purpose. David declared that his victory came from the Lord way before his victory came in the natural. In other words, he had a breakthrough in his heart and soul long before anything changed in his circumstances. You may not see it now, but there is a much bigger picture that God will open up to you in your story. Maybe it's time for a new chapter in your life. The bigger picture is how does God want to use your story? Who could he help through you? God's not done with you just because you have been through betrayals!

3. Forgive quickly

Forgiveness is a process and can sometimes take weeks, months and even several years depending on the level and depth of the betrayal. When you forgive, you are not saying that what they did is ok. No, when you forgive, it is about freeing you from the poison inside that'll keep you from moving forward and seeing the next chapter in your life.

I know it's crazy to think about forgiving the person(s) who have betrayed you, but you need to. I mean pray and forgive until you no longer want them to pay for what they have done. Ahhhhh! Now that is forgiveness. I know you may want the person(s) to pay for what they have done, forgiving them feels like you are giving them a free pass. Well, you're not! Forgiving in this context is about you removing the unnecessary baggage off of your life that someone else has placed on you. Think about this, if unforgiveness keeps you locked up in your soul, keeping you from the abundant life God promises, what kind of life could you live if you walk in forgiveness?

Jesus did a remarkable act when he forgave the people while on the cross. Right in the middle of his worst pain as a result of being betrayed, he forgave. God asks us to forgive because he forgave us. He doesn't want you locked up. Forgiving that person frees you from the hold of bitterness, anger, rage, revenge and any other thing that holds you back. Not forgiving is you taking the poison and drinking it. Forgiveness is a supernatural experience and it is the essence of Christianity. I love the fact that Christ forgave me of my sins long before I received His forgiveness. He FOR-Gave long before I knew it. One day the Apostle Peter was asking Jesus about this idea of forgiveness. He wanted to know just how far he had to go with it. What is the limit? Was it once? Seven? Read what Jesus says:

Then Peter came to Jesus and asked, "Lord, how many times shall I forgive my brother or sister who sins against me? Up to seven times?" Jesus answered, "I tell you, not seven times, but seventy times seven.
- Matt 18:21-22 (NIV)

Seriously?! 490 times?! Why such a high number? Apparently, Jesus was trying to make a point here. I believe Jesus was showing us that it is the heart of forgiveness that matters and not about just checking it off your list. I have never had someone sin against me 490 times but if they did, I'm sure it would be pretty difficult to forgive them every time. And yet, Jesus is telling us to and saying it is possible.

Forgiveness may seem impossible right now, but it can be done.

Don't carry around any extra baggage in your life because you refuse to forgive. It's your choice today that can turn the ashes of betrayal into beauty.

4. Get Back Up

You may have been blindsided or got the wind knocked out of your sails, but get back up and get going again. Continue trusting God and learn to trust others again. Love deeply again. Live your life full and in abundance...full of right relationships, peace, joy, expectation, vision and purpose. Don't let another day go by allowing someone else's betrayal, lies and accusations keep you from fulfilling what God has for you. Know that our heavenly father has not left you. You can hold onto his word and it is true. He knows where you are and his heart breaks for you; at the same time he wants to help you get to the other side of this. God can and will help you work through the mess and turn it into a message for others to read and be helped by, but you have to get back up.

You may be in the midst of the biggest mess right now, but I am confident, as you get back up, he will lead you through it. You never know how far reaching your message will go and whom it will bless. That is why you must continue walking toward health and forgiveness. I know your betrayal is painful. I know the agonizing feelings and tormenting thoughts you are experiencing, but I promise, over time you will come out golden on the other side. What could God do through your story? Who could he bless? What is next for you? What gets written in the next chapter of your life's story is up to you.

Getting beyond betrayal requires two acts on our part. The first act that is required is for us to make the decision to get up from the ashes that betrayal has left in our lives. The second requirement is that you make the decision to not let betrayal come through you. It's time we get beyond it!

13. Will you be the One?

In closing, I have some questions for you to meditate on.

First, what impact could we as the church make on the world if we made the decision to walk in humility, learn to "one-another" each other and choose unity?

What could happen if we made a decision to end betrayal within the church?

We may not be able to stop the betrayal throughout the world, but I do believe we can make an impact in our churches and our families.

In the first chapter I shared about my love and passion for the church. Even after all the churches that have been broken, my love and hope for it is even more than what it was! I am talking both the overall Big C church and the local church. I'm convinced the reason for this is that my love for Jesus and his love for me, has opened up my heart for his church. Though I once felt embarrassed by the church, I now feel hopeful, passionate and proud to be a part of it. I am passionate about seeing the local churches come alive again and fulfill their purpose. I am passionate about seeing people get beyond betrayal and fulfill God's plan for their lives.

So, here are questions for you to answer. These are for all of us who call ourselves followers of Christ.

1. Will you do your part in protecting unity?

2. Will you be the one who protects the house?

3. Will you be the one who will live clothed in humility?

4. Will you be the one who will love the church (the bride)?

5. Will you be the one who says "no more broken churches"?

6. Will you be the one who will stop being so easily offended?

7. Will you be the one who will be ok that it's not all about you?

8. Will you be the one who will forgive those who have betrayed you?

9. Will you be the one who says "Betrayal will not happen through me"?

10. Will you be the one who will pray for and cover the mistakes of others?

11. Will you be the one who will stop gossip from coming out of your mouth?

12. Will you be the one who is ok if a pastor or leader doesn't do it your way?

13. Will you be the one to stand up and say "Division will not come through me"?

14. Will you be the one who will lay down your life so that others in the body of Christ can shine?

15. Will you be the one who will use your life to "one-another" people within the church, your family and in life?

16. Will you lay down your own personal agendas, selfish ambitions and control issues so that unity can increase?

17. Will you be the one who will remain planted in a local church and become the biggest blessing to that pastor, leader and people?

18. Will you be the one who will do your part in advancing the vision and game plan of your local church so that people can be won to Jesus?

19. Will you be the one who will walk in humility and pray "Father, if there be any part of the three headed monster in me... please remove it!"

Will you be the one?

Made in the USA
Middletown, DE
09 May 2019